The
French-Inspired
Home

The
French-Inspired Home

Kaari Meng

A LARK/CHAPELLE BOOK

New York

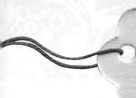

Book Editor: Catherine Risling
Art Director: Jon Zabala
Photo Stylists: Rebecca Ittner,
Kaari Meng
Photographer: Zachary Williams

A Lark/Chapelle Book

Chapelle, Ltd., Inc.
P.O. Box 9255, Ogden, UT 84409
(801) 621-2777 • (801) 621-2788 Fax
e-mail: chapelle@chapelleltd.com
Web site: www.chapelleltd.com

Created and produced by Red Lips 4 Courage Communications, Inc.
www.redlips4courage.com
Eileen Cannon Paulin
President
Catherine Risling
Director of Editorial

10 9 8 7 6 5 4 3 2 1

First Edition

Published by Lark Books, A Division of
Sterling Publishing Co., Inc.
387 Park Avenue South, New York, N.Y. 10016

The French-Inspired Home
© 2006, Kaari Meng
Photography © 2006, Lark Books
Illustrations © 2006, Melissa Easton

Distributed in Canada by Sterling Publishing,
c/o Canadian Manda Group, 165 Dufferin Street
Toronto, Ontario, Canada M6K 3H6

Distributed in the United Kingdom by GMC Distribution Services,
Castle Place, 166 High Street, Lewes, East Sussex, England BN7 1XU

Distributed in Australia by Capricorn Link (Australia) Pty Ltd.,
P.O. Box 704, Windsor, NSW 2756 Australia

Manufactured in China

ISBN 13: 978-1-57990-996-3
ISBN 10: 1-57990-996-5

For information about custom editions, special sales, premium and
corporate purchases, please contact Sterling Special Sales Department
at 800-805-5489 or specialsales@sterlingpub.com.

To Celia Rose Fitzgerald
The Creative Spirit Who Lives in All of Us

TABLE OF CONTENTS

I was first introduced to French General, a small specialty home store, when it was located in downtown Manhattan in New York City. I heard about its wonderful variety of textiles, notions, and home accessories that had a French Country sensibility. Being a devoted shopper—and editor of *Country Living*—I made the trek to see French General for myself. I wasn't disappointed.

Several years later, I heard the shop was moving to the West Coast. One week before my family and I went to Southern California for our annual December holiday I received a postcard from French General announcing their new shop in Los Angeles. I stuffed the card into my purse and made a mental note to follow up once I was in L.A. I called owner Kaari Meng two days before we were headed back to New York and she was kind enough to meet me at the shop. Once I was on the correct street, there was no doubt that the shop—located in a charming bungalow— was straight ahead. Walking into French General is walking into total comfort with wonderful textiles, books, ribbons, and home accessories all around. The shop feeds the soul and inspires you to design and create. It's a true reflection of Kaari, who continues to be immensely creative and genuine. She brings a wonderful eye to her shop and designs, along with a solid understanding of how people can use her ideas and products.

I'm so pleased to write the foreword for this book. Chapter after chapter is filled with beautiful photography along with wonderfully accessible ideas that are fresh and unique. After my L.A. visit, I immediately had French General photographed for the pages of *Country Living*. Readers responded with gusto. I'm now delighted to see Kaari have a book of her own that shows others how to incorporate vintage items into today's homes and lifestyle.

So much of what we do today is about creating moments, experiences, and memories we can share with our family and friends. Kaari's work does just that. Her handcrafted approach, along with vintage and natural materials, not only makes our homes more beautiful, but they also create a wonderful experience of combining process with creativity. I believe you'll come away from this book with the inspiration and ideas to create your own personal style in your home and to embellish what you already have and love.

Nancy Mernit Soriano
Editor in Chief
Country Living

INTRODUCTION

FRENCH GENERAL

Collecting treasures that are old, unusual, rare, and charming has been my desire for as long as I can remember. Pressed leaves, mother-of-pearl buckles, antique floral linens, ledgers written 100 years ago, French soap labels, mercury glass beads—items with a storied past to tell that have been carefully passed down through the years have been my passion for more than two decades. Estate sales, marche aux puces, and boot sales are all reasons for me to pull over and dig for old treasures.

In 1998, the precursor to my shop, French General, existed in a barn along the Hudson River filled with linen convent nighties, old pastis glasses, and antique millinery, just about anything to embellish the home and make it feel as if it had been lived in forever.

The following year I opened my first retail shop in New York City with my sister, Molly. Customers would buy glassine bags full of old elements, and they would want to know the story behind each item. Molly and I would sit for hours sharing what we knew—our provenance of an object; the cold morning we happened upon the folders of old pressed herbs at the Vanves Flea Market in Paris; how we bargained for more than an hour with the dealer, who then offered us another box of old medicinal labels for next to nothing; and how it rained and rained while we sat in a cafe for hours, talking about all of the characters who crossed our path.

All of these stories have made their way into the lives of friends and strangers, along with a bit of us and a bit of French General.

Whether Molly and I were shopping at a flea market in a field in Ohio or unearthing treasures in a basement in Paris, we brought back a way of life that had been missed, along with small bits that have been forgotten and tucked away. Our gift has been finding true souvenirs, the curiosities of a lifetime long passed.

These notions, as we have affectionately termed them, have been collected, cleaned, sorted, and stored at French General in old apothecary jars. Most were found still in their original packaging—delicate brown cardboard boxes filled with tissue and cotton, the notions carefully wrapped, waiting to be opened and enjoyed. Beads, buttons, sequins, glitter, ephemera, millinery flowers, ribbon, and feathers have all been used for making the home more decorative.

French General continues to collect and use these notions, and I encourage you to do the same. The number of ways they can be used to embellish your home is endless, and you will find dozens of our favorite ideas throughout this book.

Today French General, having switched coasts and set up shop in Los Angeles, California, is not only a source for vintage notions; it is also a workshop where household textiles, lavender bath and laundry products, and vintage craft kits are designed. We are in essence a general store for all things French. We've created a lifestyle brand based on pastimes from the turn of the last century that allows us to put our supplies to good use, as well as fill our homes—and the homes of others—with touches of French-inspired living.

ROOTED IN FRANCE

The rural traditions of France are rooted in the organic. The inspiration behind French General is my image of an old home, set amidst a pastoral landscape with a rustic country table in the dining room, an armoire filled with lavender soap in the laundry room, a bed layered with early woven textiles in the bedroom, a garden planted with herbs for cooking, and finally, a space to explore one's creative self—an atelier, sanctuary, or a studio.

These rooms existed in French homes of the last century. They were decorated with family heirlooms and collections, and filled with a sense of history and lots of embellishments. Textiles, paper, and small decorative objects were all used to make the space feel unique and like home.

Throughout this book I will show you how you can achieve this wonderful French sense of home. I'll share my knowledge of vintage notions, how to collect them, where to find them, and how I develop color palettes for decorating. I'll lead you through the French-inspired home, room by room. You will find projects you can make yourself. Some of the instructions are within the chapters and others are covered in the detailed directions in the back of the book. In the Archives section, beginning on page 102, you will find copy-ready versions of some of the ephemera I enjoy using in my own projects.

Whether you are decorating a whole house or just a room, you'll love working with organic colors, shapes, and materials—a basket full of seashells, old spools of ribbon, a tray of wooden type letters, and old mother-of-pearl buttons. Think old and timeworn, imagine the smells of lavender and citrus, and enjoy creating your own sense of home.

NOTEWORTHY
NOTIONS

A cupboard filled with notions may include antique beads, cabochons, glitter, and sequins; early millinery, ribbon, flowers, stamens, leaves, and feathers; old ephemera, dresdens, paper scraps, labels, and cards. On their own, each item might not be special or even noteworthy, but added to something or used in a project they bring a personal touch that you may have been missing. When using notions to decorate and create, think outside of the box. Try to use the item for something other than what it was intended for. The element of surprise will personalize each project you touch.

Beads can be strung to create garlands, sewn onto pillows, or displayed in jars; millinery can be used to decorate books, a piece of fabric, or worn in your hair; and old paper items are great for scrapbook pages, stationery, and even inspiration for calling cards.

Although there are all sorts of beads to collect and use, my favorites include old Japanese glass pearls, glass leaves and flowers on wire, and nail-head glass, typically flat-backed on one side and faceted on the top. I also adore French bugle beads, which can be up to 4" long and usually have ribbed edges; mercury glass, hollow glass beads that have been lined with silver; and finally, old glass rings.

I make good use out of cabochons, flat-backed notions that can be set into a prong setting or glued into a bezel typically used for rings, earrings, and pendants. Some of the ways I like to use cabochons include the postcard garland featured in Chapter 1. High-domed and pressed-flower cabochons are my favorites.

A collection of old Japanese glass pearls in botanical shapes are gathered and displayed to form a collection.

Old millinery stamens and flowers are arranged on a handmade shelf originally used to display dyes.

Millinery flowers are made from starched fabric pressed into molds. The petals are then sewn or glued together to construct a specific flower. A stem with stamens attached is added to hold the flower together. The stamens are set in the middle of the flower for a focal point—a place to rest the eyes. Stamens are made out of almost any material: papier-mâché, glass, clay, and jewels. Leaves can also be added to give the effect that the flower has just been picked from a branch. Velvet and paper leaves come in all shapes and colors. Collecting old millinery flowers is a charming way to bring the outside in and fill your home with blooms all year round.

Antique glass glitter adds a touch of antiquity to any project. Keep your eyes open for different sized glitter shards. Very fine and medium fine glitter can give a different effect to each project.

Sequins were originally used as a decorative sewing element, hand sewn one by one. They are a labor of love on any piece of clothing. Sequins with holes can be sewn onto cloth, paper, or even glued onto most surfaces. Sequins come as small as 1mm and as large as 25mm. There are also some interesting two-sided celluloid sequins that tend to melt when they are washed in hot water due to the old plastic.

Velvet, grosgrain, rayon, satin, or silk ribbon come in almost every color imaginable and can be used on everything from wrapped gift boxes to bookmarks. Typically available in at least five different widths, you can also dig for 6" black grosgrain that was used on men's hats during Queen Victoria's mourning period, pre-1900s.

Jars of vintage beads are labeled with glass letter beads that form a small garland.

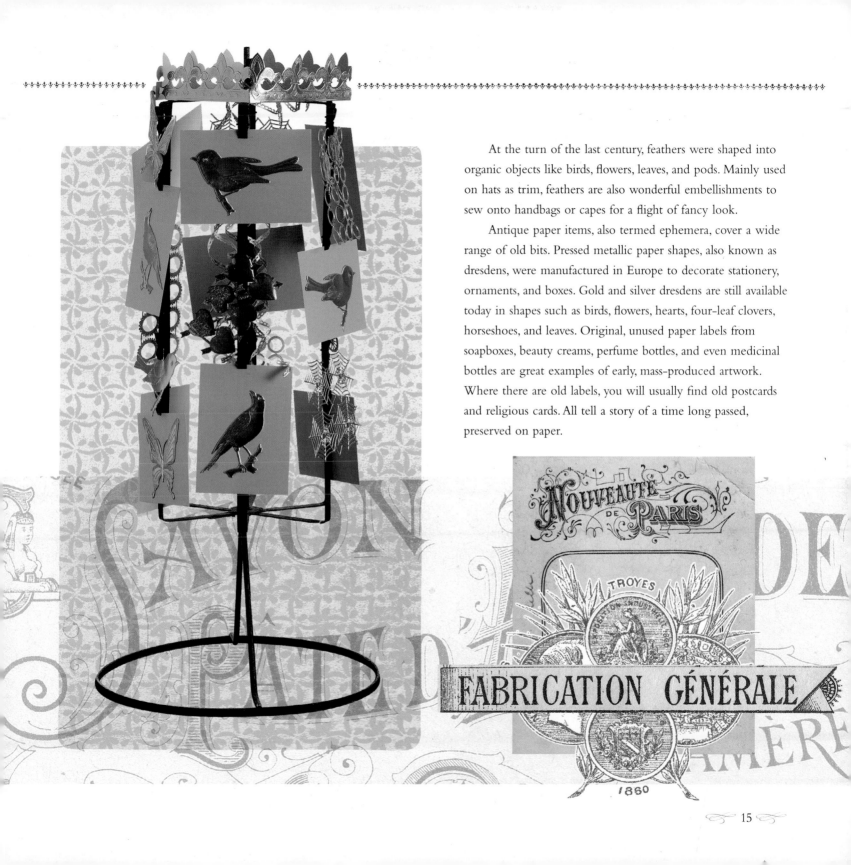

At the turn of the last century, feathers were shaped into organic objects like birds, flowers, leaves, and pods. Mainly used on hats as trim, feathers are also wonderful embellishments to sew onto handbags or capes for a flight of fancy look.

Antique paper items, also termed ephemera, cover a wide range of old bits. Pressed metallic paper shapes, also known as dresdens, were manufactured in Europe to decorate stationery, ornaments, and boxes. Gold and silver dresdens are still available today in shapes such as birds, flowers, hearts, four-leaf clovers, horseshoes, and leaves. Original, unused paper labels from soapboxes, beauty creams, perfume bottles, and even medicinal bottles are great examples of early, mass-produced artwork. Where there are old labels, you will usually find old postcards and religious cards. All tell a story of a time long passed, preserved on paper.

COLLECTING IN QUANTITY

For as long as I can remember, I've collected old items in quantity. I have always been drawn to boxes full of chenille leaves, glass flower cabochons, and button cards. Having just one would not satisfy me; a gross, mass, or kilo—once I unearthed the gem, I bought the boxful.

Hand-curled feathers, orange blossom wax flowers, and hand-pulled Japanese glass leaves were all used in abundance at the turn of the last century, when people took the time to embellish their lives, clothes, and homes.

Throughout this book we show you our collections and what we have created with these notions. We list the items and supplies used, though you can replicate our ideas with findings of your own. Remember, uncovering gold does not happen on the first dig; it usually turns up after years of searching and uncovering layers and layers of dust and dirt.

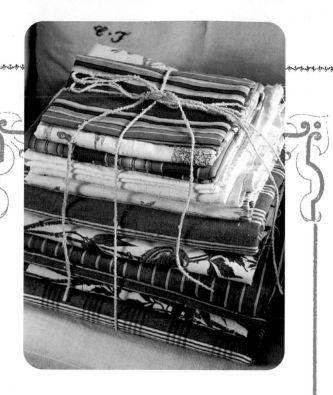

INSPIRATIONS

❧ TIPS ON COLLECTING ❧

- Add to your collections whenever you can. When you see it, buy it if you can afford it.
- Always collect something that speaks to you.
- Collect something you haven't seen before; you'll have a better chance of finding more.
- Display your collections by color. Pieces look richer and are easier to display together, even if you don't have a large grouping.
- Recycle old collections that don't mean as much to you. This will give you the capital to buy your next collection.

PLACES TO SHOP

My favorite places to collect are estate sales, flea markets, and, dare I say, online. At estate sales, I look for old sewing notions, early photo books, laundered handkerchiefs—just about anything at the back of an old closet. Estate sales are usually listed in the local paper a day or so before the sale. Many estate sale dealers have a mailing list, so be sure to add your name and you will be given early notice for the next sale.

Estate sales are typically great places to learn about other collectors and you'll see plenty of their collections including household textiles, jewelry, craft supplies, and loads of old photographs. You may find, for example, a trunk full of hats from the 1950s covered with old millinery flowers. Buying the whole collection may get you a better deal, as buying in quantity does have its advantages. Even if you are not a hat collector, the vintage silk and velvet flowers can be used on top of a beautifully wrapped package or on your inspiration board.

At flea markets, I search out early rural textiles, religious medals, paintings, and ephemera. If you are lucky enough to buy at flea markets in Europe you will see much older collections. Books and paintings from the 17th, 18th, and 19th centuries are quite common. Molly and I have always been drawn to old papers: ledgers, photo books, labels, anything with printed matter on them. The old type on these pieces can be a great addition to your journals and collages.

On the Internet, I look for old, odd groupings from 100 years ago that are being sold off by a distant relative. There are all sorts of auctions and antique sites to explore. Try using your favorite search engine with key words such as early paper, antique textiles, and old collection (of a particular item). These specific searches should turn up an interesting selection of items.

INSPIRATIONS

❧ SHOPPING FLEA MARKETS ❧

When embarking on a hunt for treasures, keep in mind the following:

- **GET UP EARLY**. Hit the market as the sun is rising. In the early morning, dealers are usually still unpacking. Everyone is chatting, welcoming each other, and if you're lucky, offering hot tea from a thermos. By your second walk through, dealers begin to recognize you and may invite you into their booths.

- **TAKE A NOTEBOOK.** Scribble down prices as you peruse. If you don't speak the language, having the dealer write down the asking price is a great way to communicate. Then try crossing out the price and asking for a lower price; the dealer may return the favor by scratching out the offer and writing one in between, which is still lower than the original asking price.

- **LOOK FOR UNIQUE THINGS.** Uncommon, rare, and unique purchases always add character to a home. My favorites are old herbiers, early sewing baskets (better if they are filled), old journals, autograph books, small paintings (especially in pairs), and any sort of household textile in good shape.

- **EAT AT THE FLEA MARKET.** This sounds like a basic idea, but you'll be surprised that, before you know it, it's already noon. I always feel better after I eat. My decisions are sharper and if you get dehydrated in the middle of a flea market jaunt, nothing is fun.

- **DON'T FORGET THE WET WIPES.** These are nice to have on hand to clean your hands after looking through piles of old pottery, black-and-white photographs, and other flea market items.

- **BRING A CARRYALL.** If you have a carrier or cart with wheels, bring it. Rather than walking around with many bags, fill your carrier and wheel it behind you. It will also keep your hands free to explore your next great find.

COLOR PALETTES

Color is an important part of the French-inspired home. One of the keys to decorating with color is to first be inspired by color. The best way to be inspired by color is to look outside. Teach yourself to see the interesting color combinations in nature. The pink and red swirled sunset or the indigo and teal ocean waves give us an impressive spectrum of all of the shades of color in between.

This book is not only organized by rooms in a home, but by colors within each room—all different shades of pinks, blues, reds, greens, and natural hues. Color preferences are subjective so find the color palette that suits you and your many moods best. I tend to favor the colors I imagine filling an old house—worn dusty colors that are deep and vibrant.

Finding a color palette that makes you feel comfortable takes time and patience—and a lot of experimenting. Try keeping a color book where you paste down color inspirations—cards, ribbon, photographs—any small item that will help you create your own palette.

Once you have found a shade of a color you are comfortable with, start experimenting with other colors within the same saturation. If you love the palest petal pink shade, try layering it with a soft turquoise or different shades of sage, fern, or lily green.

Your color palette can be inspired thematically by nature, seasons, fabrics, architecture, and so on. My favorite muses are flora and fauna. I collect vintage fabrics and postcards and often pull from the colors found in these items. Then I add new colors to complete the palette. The possibilities are endless and I can spend hours playing with variations. At some point I do have to narrow the choices down and typically end up with one main color and three complementary hues.

THE CREATIVE SPACE

We painted our creative space plume bleu, which is a very soft turquoise color, because it inspires my creative desires. The color is soft enough to invite relaxation, yet bold enough to stir imaginative energies to compose pretty things. Much of the jewelry I design has elements of turquoise and coral in each piece so this seemed like the natural color for my room. The rosy pink and pale red elements throughout the room—from the draperies to the glass-filled apothecary jars—encourage beauty and thought.

THE BEDROOM

The bedroom, although fully clothed in shades of red, is simple and not too feminine. This is a place for both my husband and me, so I keep in mind dark wood furnishings that coexist with my favorite colors. By mixing red textiles with mossy green paint on the walls we created an informal space that can be used for relaxing and entertaining as well as sleeping. Layering this room was important so you'll find every nook filled with subtle shades of red, pink, and green.

THE DINING ROOM

Oatmeal hues, steel indigo blues, and warm, rustic taupe are the dining room colors. This room gets a lot of natural light so the calm, soothing colors make the room seem alive and inviting. The textiles we use in this room are also natural—nubby hemp, linen, and nettle along with madder-striped grain bags. The hues of these fabrics inspire our palette. Natural hen eggs blend well with creamy yellow beeswax sheets to create a sense of history and warmth in this room.

PILULES DE SANTÉ

pour pigeons, poules et autres
animaux de basse-cour.

Préviennent et guérissent
toutes les maladies
de la
volaille

HAND
WASHABLE

WILLS'S CIGARETTES.

SMALL WHITE

INDUSTRIE FRANÇAISE

FABRIQUE
DE BAGUETTE
DORE

ENCADREMENTS & TENTURES

LLE · FR

SAIN

dés par

(VOS

THE LAUNDRY ROOM

The image of an old French laundry room
inspired us to paint our room a washed stone
color with accents of indigo and natural linen.
White is typically considered such a sterile
choice, but mix in the hues of natural fibers
and a dash of color and you have a winning
combination. Blue elicits a sense of serenity
and cleanliness in this room, making it much
more of a work room than just a place to
wash household laundry.

THE GARDEN

It's so easy—and some say advisable—to borrow from Mother Nature's hues when planting and decorating in the garden. No other color but green dominates the scene, yet the support performers can nearly steal the show. Add in the wonderful hues of lavender, sage, and a lemon or two and you can't go wrong mixing and matching colors. This space encourages the naturalist in me to come out so I surround myself with all different botanical patterns in organic shades of green, brown, and natural.

objets memorables

CHAPTER 1

The Creative Space

Everyone needs a creative space, a place to build, make, transform, or to do nothing at all. Color, imagination, inspiration, and a sense of organization are all elements that define one's own creative space. It doesn't have to be a large space, just an area to escape to and discover where your creative thread may take you.

My very first creative space was set up behind an old wooden screen in a one-bedroom apartment on 20th Street in New York City. My husband, Jon, and I had found a drafting table on the street and this became my desk, which I lined with jars of old beads I was beginning to collect. I organized all of the beads by shades of color so eventually my creations started to naturally revolve around unique color combinations that I seemed to discover whenever I sat down to design.

This was a great inspiration and eye opener for me. I had never realized there were so many shades of one color. I remember Roy G. Biv, the acronym I learned in fourth grade to remember the order of colors in a rainbow—red, orange, yellow, green, blue, indigo, and violet.

After months of looking, thinking, and experimenting with the glass beads, I designed a line of hatpins that I eventually sold to Bergdorf Goodman department store in New York City. What an exciting day that was for me! Selling treasures that come out of your creative space is the ultimate stamp of approval for a meandering artist.

The creative space allows you to pursue your craft and develop your own style in an inspiring atmosphere.

FINDING YOUR OWN SPACE

Creative spaces change depending upon one's needs.
When I was designing hatpins years ago, I was
content with a desk and a handful of jars that held
the beads and pins. I didn't use many tools but
I stocked all sorts of bead glue and epoxy. Then I
started my own line of vintage glass jewelry and
I needed a different set up, one with more room for
designing, an inspiration board to show color trends,
and a lot more apothecary jars for the ever-growing
collection of vintage beads I was accumulating.

Whether your creative space is at home, in an
old barn, or in the garage, hang up anything that
inspires you: photographs, strands of beads, button
cards, and ribbon swatches. Organize your collections
so that you can rest your eyes on something
inspiring every day. Let your passions emerge.

A creative space is a place to draw, paint, write,
knit, bead, paste, and think. Listen to your heart
and let your imagination help you fashion an
environment that allows your creative energy to flow.

Whether your creative space
is at home, in an old barn,
or in the garage, hang up
anything that inspires you.

ORGANIZING

Like collecting, organizing can be done by color so that the organization itself makes a good-looking collection. For years my sister, Molly, has collected a certain shade of aqua-green pottery, all manufactured before the 1940s. The company that made each piece is less important than the color. Displayed together, this collection is quite impressive because the subtle shades of the palette are easily seen and appreciated.

In our shop we have a space we call the notions room. Each collection has its own area and its own system for organizing. Here you'll find old apothecary jars filled with vintage millinery, beads, and buttons.

Everything is arranged by color, which is especially helpful when designing with particular hues in mind. Our storage closet is filled with drawers and bins arranging all of our stock by color and type. Beads are in one drawer, cabochons in another. Not only does this allow me to see what I've collected over the years, it's also easy to see how much stock of a notion I have before I use it in a kit or a piece of jewelry.

Vintage paper and delicate collections are kept in an 18th-century optician case. Filled with more than a dozen glass-fronted drawers, the case is a wonderful way to store anything that needs to be flat. Once again, each drawer is arranged by color so black-and-white medicinal labels are kept next to black antique lace gloves wrapped in brown paper. Glass glitter and French sequins are stored in old French jelly jars. These are small bits and it's nice to have them all in one place.

Many find labeling their storage to be useful. Making small labels with the name of the item, the price you paid, and where you bought it can be helpful if you ever need to order more or simply want to keep track of your collection. If you can't find your own vintage labels, we've provided some for you to reproduce (see Archives, pages 102-113).

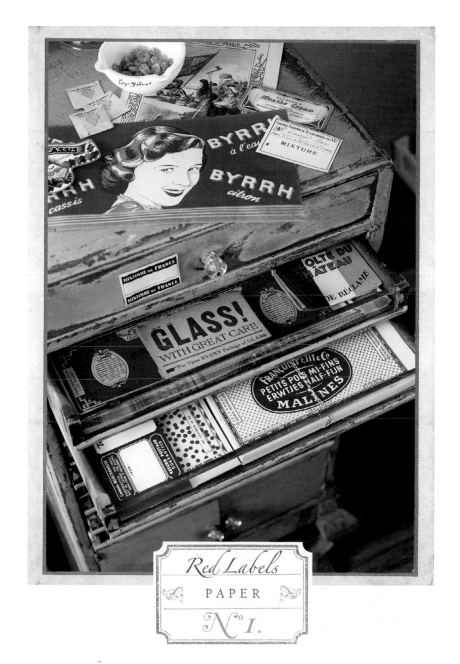

Red Labels

PAPER

N.º I.

BEADED LIGHT COVERS

My good friend, Suzan Etkin, has been designing and blowing glass in Italy for more than 25 years. One summer she started designing these light bulb covers out of small semi-precious beads, inspired by her mother's collection of antique crystal covers. The beaded-glass covers completely surround the bulb and are similar to vintage bulb covers made in the 1920s and imported from Europe. Sue designs her covers to sparkle when the lights are on and serve as a decorative home accent when the lights are off.

To make a beaded light cover, cut strips of wire to fit around your light bulb. You will also need a top and bottom wire to hold all of the strips into place. Once you cut the wire, string beads along each piece using a pattern that will let the light shine through. Crystals and soft colors like light pink, light amber, and opal are perfect beads to use to make beaded covers. These covers can be fitted to the bulbs on a chandelier or a single bulb that hangs from an old light fixture.

BUTTON BOXES

Many times I will buy an old sewing basket filled with buttons, dozens of some and just one of others. I will often separate these into piles by their kind: mother-of-pearl, glass, celluloid, and Bakelite. Once categorized, I store them in small boxes.

This is a practical way to store your collection of buttons so that you can see what is inside of each box. Paint a small cardboard or papier-mâché box and glue a label onto the lid. If you don't have an old label, we've provided a few favorites (see Archives, pages 102-113).

Once the label is dry, glue one of each button stored inside on top of the lid. Keep this collection close by; you'll be surprised how often you can use buttons to embellish your projects and home. Sew buttons onto pillows and bed covers, or change out the buttons on your favorite sweater every once in a while for a new look.

POSTCARD GARLAND

For as long as I can remember, I have collected postcards simply for the beauty of the card and stored them in an old wire basket. I pick them up at museum gift shops, antique shops, airports, and flea markets. As long as they inspire me, I buy them.

It's like a trip down memory lane whenever I look through them. Some are copies of paintings by Cezanne while others are sepia-tone photographs of San Sebastian, a northern town in Spain. I still rummage through the basket to find one to send on special birthdays to friends, although the majority is difficult for me to part with. It is important for a collector to accumulate favorite things; a collector is a modern version of the hunter-gatherer.

Nearly every home during the early part of the 20th century had a postcard album filled with greetings. Students presented them to teachers, faraway relatives used them to keep in touch, and an occasional beau would profess his love for his lady with a beautifully decorated card.

We use old postcards and vintage-inspired cards to decorate special packages and make into garlands. Many of the elements that were used to decorate postcards at the turn of the last century are still available today, including glass glitter, mica, tinsel, feathers, French sequins, and flat-back cabochons.

Have fun with the image itself. Add feathers, cabochons, or tiny mother-of-pearl buttons for a baby card. Cutting or deckling the edges will make the card look and feel old. Be sure to present your card in a glassine or vellum envelope to give it a truly vintage feel, or you can thread old ribbon through each card and hang them as a decorative garland in your creative space.

To make your own postcard garland, begin with images that inspire you to embellish. They could be old postcards found at a flea market or new images you created and then color-copied. Use a fine-tip glue pen to write on the card and then sprinkle on glass glitter or a very fine sparkly powder. Mica works well as it adheres to glue and really makes your message stand out.

(See Instructions, page 114.)

TOOL KIT WRAPS

Tools make what we do more productive; they are the cornerstones of all craft projects, and they make our work easier. Keeping them close at hand, protected, and organized is an invaluable investment in time.

Whether it's jewelry tools, knitting needles, sewing needles, or paintbrushes, all creative implements should be well cared for so they are ready for the next project. Think of your tools as the means to allowing you to create; without them it is difficult to produce much of anything.

An easy way to carry small tools is to wrap them in a fabric roll with at least three to four pockets, and a ribbon to tie it closed. We have found two roll sizes useful: A shorter roll is perfect for smaller jewelry or crochet tools, while a longer wrap with a flap is ideal for knitting needles or paintbrushes.

Choose durable fabric like canvas for your tool kit wrap. You want them to protect your tools for a long time. We used natural hemp, one of the oldest and strongest materials known to man, for our wraps. For the sewing needles we used cotton and felt, which makes it easy to sew on extra buttons and slide in needles.

DECORATIVE PUSHPINS
& MAGNETS

Collecting old bits and pieces comes easy to many of us. The challenge is utilizing this ever-growing collection without having to store it away for someone else to find in 100 years.

Pull out your button collection and make simple magnets or pushpins for your inspiration board. Hot glue magnets onto the backs of buttons. We embellished ours with mother-of-pearl buttons, cabochons, and crystals. You could also use buttons to create a frame around a photograph that is adhered onto a magnet sheet.

Try layering your pieces. Glue the largest button in place first and then add smaller pieces on top of it. Old game pieces, like bingo markers or checkers, make interesting magnets as well.

Next time you come across a small bag of old sewing notions, look for thimbles or spools of thread; they all have a flat bottom surface that would easily adhere to a magnet. Just be sure the magnet is strong enough to support the weight. Craft stores usually stock different kinds of magnets, including penny-size discs and strips.

INSPIRATION BOARD

Posting beautiful photographs and fond memories is an inspiring way to fill a memory board, or inspiration board, as we call it. Many artists adorn their boards with color swatches, ribbons, quotes, photographs, ticket stubs, or notes from friends.

For the cover of your board, choose an heirloom handkerchief, a piece of fabric from a dress worn long ago, or a tablecloth that can no longer be used due to stains or holes. Then find a ribbon or trim that complements the colors of the fabric, and finally, search your sewing basket for a handful of buttons to be added where the ribbon crosses itself to provide another layer of texture.

Hang your inspiration board near your desk and tuck in ideas, photographs of a faraway destination, a dried flower, and maybe even an old compass—just about any piece that will guide you through your creative moments.

(See Instructions, page 114.)

SHELF PAPER

Shelf paper can be used to line dresser drawers or to soften the shelf edges of an armoire or wall shelf. Typically, French paper was scalloped and had tiny designs printed on it. Cherries, checks, and flowers all made for pretty paper designs.

Years ago, my sister and I stumbled upon a huge stock of vintage French shelf paper at our favorite antique kitchen shop in the Marais area of Paris and we've been using it ever since. But all good things must come to an end and our stock is running out. So we decided to re-create the look of old paper using new and vintage materials.

Old paper is extremely delicate so we chose to use new, printed paper, which is actually fabric color copied with a scallop cut along the bottom edge. We decorated the paper by piercing it with a tiny crochet needle every 1" then weaving ribbon through the holes and adhering sequins or cabochons with craft glue.

To make your own French-inspired shelf paper, take measurements of the shelf you want to cover. Cut your paper so you have enough left to fold over the top edge of the shelf, then either cut a scalloped edge or leave it straight. Once you have a pattern established for the edging, continue cutting all the way down the length of the paper. Embellish to your heart's content with beads, ribbon, rhinestones, or whatever else strikes a creative chord.

PRETTY IN PAINT

After searching for the perfect colors to paint the 1926 Spanish bungalow that houses French General, we decided to create our own palette. Our paint is made for us by a friend whose family has owned Catalina Paints in Los Angeles for more than 40 years. The paint for French General is hemp-based and has a low gloss, silky-sheen texture, which is perfect for walls, furniture, and craft projects.

Paint consists of pigments, resin, and binder. The proportion of pigment to binder in any paint dictates the amount of gloss the finished product will have. Generally, the glossier the finish, the more hard wearing it will be.

There are various categories of finish: matte, gloss, and a range between the two, which varies according to the manufacturer. Some common finishes include flat, eggshell, silk, satin, semi-gloss, and high gloss.

Water-based paint dries purely by evaporation. The greatest advantage of water-based paint is that brushes and rollers can be washed out in water; no special cleaning solution is needed.

When you paint the rooms in your home, choose colors that make you feel relaxed and allow you to breathe easily. A light-filled room with softly colored walls allows you to grow creatively and inspires your projects and artwork. If you aren't sure which colors to use, pick a few different hues in quart sizes and paint large squares on two different walls. Live with these colors for a few days and see how the daylight affects them.

Keep paint samples in old glass jars close by for quick touch ups or to add to projects that need some color.

GIFT-WRAPPING STATION

Enjoy wrapping a gift as much as giving the gift. Wrapping a gift can be a pleasure if you have all of your materials stored in one place. Design a wrapping station that stores all of your paper, ribbons, tags, and small charms, as well as scissors and tape. Having everything in one place makes it easier to see what you have on hand to wrap a pretty package.

My husband built a shelf to hold boxes and rolls of paper on top and a ribbon rod underneath. If you hang a shelf over a small worktable, you can store your scissors and other essentials in the drawers of the table or on top in small containers. Recycled gift bags, tissue, and ribbons can all be kept in baskets underneath the table for easy access.

INSPIRATIONS

❧ SIMPLE DESIGNS ❧

Form, color, and texture are all essential elements in the simple process of design. I think this can only be learned through much practice and the belief that what comes out of you is your design—therefore, it is good design. If we constantly compare ourselves to other artists and strive to design like them we will lose sight of our own creative soul. Start by adding a little bit of yourself to everything you do, whether it's making a collage, sending a handmade card, or wrapping a present in an interesting way.

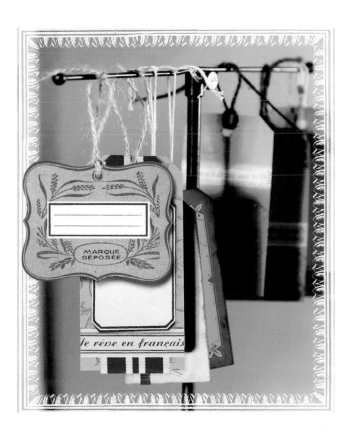

INSPIRATIONS

❧ GIFT WRAPPING ❧
SUPPLIES

To make wrapping gifts a cinch, stock your station with the following:

- Bone folder (to create smooth edges)
- Double-sided permanent tape
- Glue dots (to keep ribbons in place)
- Sharp paper scissors and/or fabric scissors

To make your own tags you'll need:

- Embossing powder and heat gun
- Eyelets and eyelet-setting tools
- Inkpads for stamping and inking edges of tags
- Thin ribbons
- Various stamps such as birds, flowers, and alphabet letters

WRAPPING GIFTS

I remember my dad showing me how to wrap a present years ago. At the time I couldn't understand why his presents always looked so perfect and mine were covered with all sorts of bits of tape and scrawny ribbon. I can recall how he folded under the ends so there weren't any raw edges and then used just one piece of tape per end. Sure enough, because of an old skill learned years ago, I now love wrapping presents and find a great thrill in handmade paper, decorative ribbon, and the perfect pair of scissors.

To wrap a beautiful present, always start with a piece of paper that is interesting, whether it's the Sunday comics, a delicate piece of handmade paper, or a sheet of tinfoil. With paper scissors, cut the sheet so there is enough paper to fold over all of the edges, and then wrap the paper around the box. Tape down on either end as well as the middle seam. Choose a ribbon that complements the paper and tie it around the gift, into a bow.

A simple handmade tag or millinery flower can be used to top off the present. Tags come in all shapes and sizes, as illustrated on page 47. If you can't find one that's just right, consider making your own out of cardstock with a paper punch or stencil. For a vintage feel, rub the edges of the tag along a brown inkpad.

A beautifully wrapped gift is a reflection of the giver and can be a simple way to express your gratitude or join in a celebration.

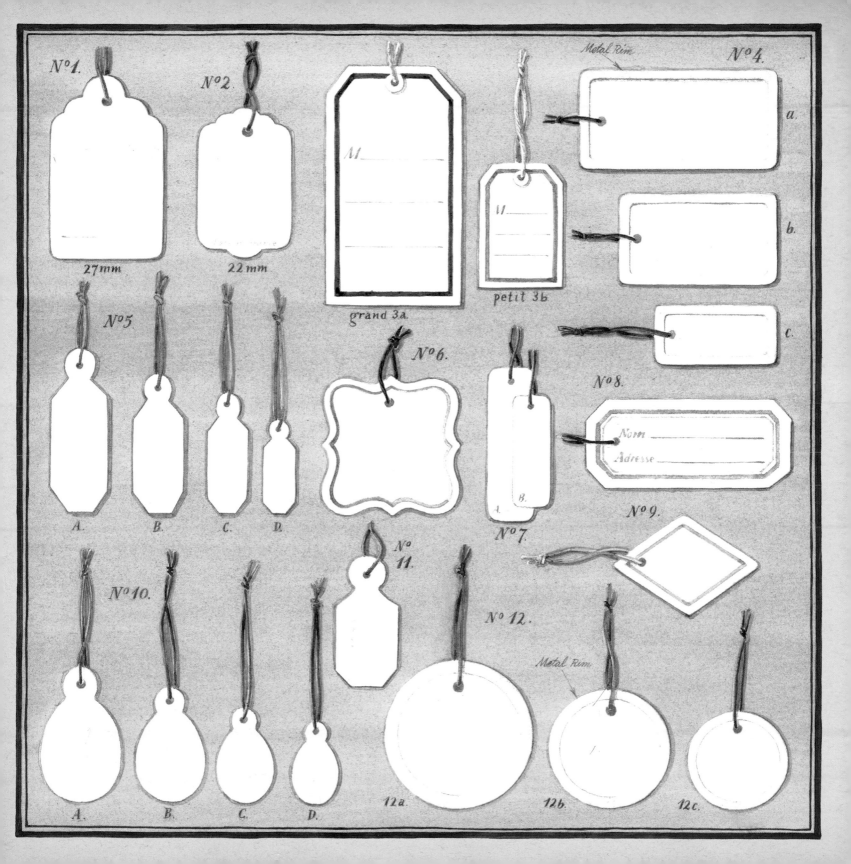

Bon Appétit

The Dining Room

> "It's surprising how much memory is built around things unnoticed at the time."
> —*Barbara Kingsolver*

The dining room is one of those magical rooms where you can alter the décor as often as you like by simply changing table linens, china, glassware, or flatware. I like to mix old and new in the dining room—vintage textiles and silver-plated flatware are at home with newly made place cards and etched glassware.

When it came to collecting dinnerware, a friend's mother, who was an antiques dealer, always recommended, "No chips." This is a good rule to live by so that when you set the table each piece is in good enough shape to eat off or serve from.

My roommate in college, Dominique Lemaire, is one of five sisters, all of whom live in Paris. Whenever we are able to visit, Dominique and her sisters put on easy, elegant dinner parties to welcome us to their city. The table is set with a mix of old silver and china from their mother as well as new textiles from Sainte Maxime in the south of France, where they spend their summers.

A meal would not be complete without five full courses, ending with a dessert of cheese and fruit, all presented on elegant serving pieces. It is a French tradition to gather around the table and sit for a full meal and then sit some more for a discussion of films, politics, and usually a bit of religion. There is such an ease with which they entertain and serve a dinner. Dominique and her family have taught me to enjoy the time around a dining table as well as the conversation.

CARING FOR VINTAGE LINENS

When caring for and storing old linens, keep in mind the following:

- Determine whether fabric should be hand washed. Anything with small detailing such as hand stitching should be soaked in lukewarm water and cleaned with powdered soap.

- Using a washing machine is perfectly acceptable when cleaning heavier fabrics; just be sure to use mild detergent on the cold water cycle and a whitener. Select the quickest and most gentle wash cycle.

- After the machine goes through its deep rinse, rinse again to remove detergent from the fabrics. Add ¼ to ½ cup of white vinegar during the final rinse cycle.

- If possible, line dry linens to retain color and preserve delicate fabrics.

- When using a machine dryer, use the permanent press cycle.

- Iron only if linen is to be used right away. Use two or three towels on the ironing board in addition to a standard pad. For added crispness, use spray-on starch. For scented linens, spray on distilled water mixed with a few drops of essential oil.

- Between uses, store linens in a white cotton pillowcase. This protects them from bright light and dust. Wash pillowcases several times, even if new, to make sure dyes and other preservatives are removed.

- Store linens at room temperature; avoid attics and basements.

TEXTILES FOR THE TABLE

Fresh, white linen napkins are among my most favorite things. I've been collecting them for years and am constantly amazed at how well they hold up, if taken care of properly. Recently I started making new napkins to add to my collection, either out of white linen or natural summer hemp. With regular use, these fabrics age gracefully and look like vintage fabric. When sewing a set of napkins, cut nice, large squares—at least 18" x 18"—so the cloth covers the lap comfortably.

Monograms are a classic way to decorate table linens and most embroidery houses have a variety of typefaces and colors to choose from. Sometimes I have napkins monogrammed with a single initial, either in the corner or in the center of the napkin. You may want to keep your eye out for old linen tablecloths and simply have these embroidered with your initials or family monogram.

Once you have a set of napkins, you will want to add more textiles to your table to really soften the surface. Layer with one color or within similar color tones to give your table a more inviting look. Choose placemats first and then try a tablecloth or a runner. Start simple and then slowly embellish according to the holiday or event.

I like using an old hemp sheet as a tablecloth and then layering textiles that are a shade lighter or darker. French tea towels with indigo or madder strips are the perfect size for making two placemats. Simply cut the towel in half and sew a hemp or heavier linen onto the back. By reinforcing the back of the cloth, these will hold up for years to come.

If you happen upon a piece of fabric that is long and narrow, consider making a table runner. Hem the four sides and lay on top of your tablecloth, then set the table with the placemats and napkins. This cloth will keep your tablecloth cleaner. Add antique silver flatware and some simple water and wine glasses and you have set a table that could have been in a St. Rémy home at the turn of the last century.

(See Instructions, page 114.)

Sometimes I have napkins monogrammed with a single initial, either in the corner or in the center of the napkin.

ETCHED GLASSES

One year my sister and I went to Brimfield, the famous flea market in Massachusetts, to buy for our shop in New York. I found two sets of old drinking glasses, one I paid way too much for and the other I paid almost nothing for. I couldn't part with either set, and they are still used daily in our home.

One is a set of old advertising glasses, probably from a turn-of-the-last-century bar, that reads "Richardson's Real Orangeade." The other set consists of champagne glasses delicately etched with polka dots and leaves. These glasses are examples of the type of wonderful glasswork manufactured and etched by hand by many of the smaller glass companies in the United States and in Europe in the 1920s.

To reproduce this elegant style of etched glassware, start with a simple design like polka dots, stripes, or a single initial. Once you have chosen your design, make a stencil out of a thin, flexible sheet of plastic. Next, find some old glasses at a garage sale or hardware store. Try to find at least four to six glasses so you will end up with a set. With double-sided tape, adhere the stencil onto the glass and gently brush on etching glass cream following the manufacturer's directions. Let cream sit 5 minutes then rinse the glass well under water, peel off the stencil, and repeat the process on the remaining glasses.

We've provided templates you can copy (see Archives, pages 102–113), or you can use any of the flexible stencils sold at most craft stores.

(See Instructions, page 115.)

INSPIRATIONS

❧ CLEANING YOUR ❧ GLASSWARE

My parents have always entertained in great style. Whether it's a dinner party for eight or a grand soiree for 100, my dad typically follows a night of entertaining with a routine of hand washing the old glasses and stemware. He never puts any of the pieces in the dishwasher, as the salts and detergents could harm the surface and cause cloudiness. He washes the glasses carefully in a plastic bowl with a towel or foam mat on the bottom using warm water and a little liquid soap, one piece at a time. If the glass is very dirty or greasy, he adds a few drops of household ammonia to the water, unless the piece is gilded.

Each glass is dried carefully and thoroughly while it is still warm by using a lint-free cloth—old linen tea towels are perfect for this as they don't shed. A warm hair dryer can also be used, well away from the sink and water, to dry the inside of a decanter. Or, place the glass vessels upside down in an airing cupboard for 24 hours. You can also roll up a paper towel, push it into a decanter until it touches the bottom, being careful not to lose the end, and remove it 24 hours later.

If your glasses appear dull, try adding a little salt to the water as dullness is caused by hard water; the harder the water the more likely the glassware is to appear cloudy.

GUEST BOOK

When I first moved to New York, I lived with a wonderful roommate who worked as a personal assistant to actress Patricia Neal. Every once in a while, Patricia would invite us over for drinks and then treat us to dinner at an Upper East Side French steakhouse. One of my fondest memories is arriving at Patricia's home and looking through her guest book, which sat on her entrance table and was always filled with her most recent visitors. I would read through all sorts of names I recognized and then add my name and a short note in the book. I thought it was a wonderful idea to have everyone who visits your home sign his or her name, whether to record dinner parties, special occasions, or simply friends who stop by for a chat.

This is a project where you can finally use all those bits of ephemera that mean something to you and will be preserved in a book for years to come. To make your guest book special, design pages with pictures that remind you of family events or use vintage sepia-tone photographs of people eating or preparing food together. Old autograph books are another great source of quirky and funny greetings that make for interesting pages. Include a photograph or menu of a special dinner in the pages of your book to remind you of each gathering.

(See Instructions, page 115.)

Soirée

HAND-ROLLED CANDLES

No dining room is complete without candles and candlelight. Early candles were made with ropes of dried vegetable fibers, sticks, or flax threads dipped in pitch, saturated fats, natural resins, tar, wax, or a combination of the latter. When resinous woods were scarce, the pith of rushes, reeds, and grasses were used as wicks.

Luckily, candle making has become quite a bit easier in recent years. Rolling beeswax sheets requires no heat, which makes it convenient for those with limited space or time.

Beeswax sheets seem to roll best in normal room temperature. If the wax is too cold it will not roll well and may crack, or at the very least not stick to itself. If the wax is too warm it will be too soft to roll. The pattern on the wax will become flattened while rolling and even your fingers will leave unsightly dents in the candles. My brother, Michael, rolls his candles outside in the sun for just the right amount of heat.

The most important thing when rolling beeswax candles is to make good contact between the wick and the wax, allowing no space between the two. Therefore, the first roll is the most important. Press the wax into the wick on all sides, watching the shape as you roll. Spread your fingers across the length of the candle for even rolling. Press the outer edge into the candle and seal the seam by applying a heated butter knife carefully to the surface.

MENU CARDS & PLACE CARDS

Several years ago, when my sister, Molly, and I would travel to Paris on buying trips for French General, we visited a small village in the Marais region called Saint-Paul. There was an old shop there called L'Ivre D'Antan on Rue de L'Ave-Maria, owned by Maurice and his lovely wife, Caroline. The basement of their shop was filled with old paper labels and cards and we would bring suitcases full of original early French artwork back to New York.

I remember the menu cards most from these basement digs. They were embellished with the most beautiful hand-painted artwork. I saved quite a few of these cards and still use them to write out dinner menus when we have a special gathering of friends for a meal. Menu cards have traditionally been utilized to list all of the items available on a given night in a restaurant. You can use them at home to let guests know what you will be serving at a dinner party.

Taking inspiration from these old menu cards, we designed a couple of templates you can color copy onto heavy cardstock and then cut to a proper size, usually 5" x 8" (see Archives, pages 102–113). After hand coloring or color copying the cards, embellish with glitter, ribbons, or seed beads to add a vintage look.

Place cards are another easy way to add your personal touch to a table setting. They are used for directing guests to a particular seat at your table. To create your own place cards, cut heavy cardstock into 3" x 4" sheets, then score or fold the card so they form a 3" x 2" tent. Another place card project is to select an image, cut it out, and adhere it to a ready-made place card base. Use your place cards to set a theme around your table.

(See Instructions, page 116.)

INSPIRATIONS

❧ COLLECTING ❧
INTERESTING EPHEMERA

- Books—Autograph books, cash books, diaries, inventory books, journals, ledgers.
- Cards—Business cards, postcards, trade cards.
- Catalogues and brochures—Agriculture books, fabric samples, seed books.
- Early receipts—Bank deposits, gas bills, grain deliveries, worker's compensation.
- Labels—Luggage, perfume, shipping, soap, wine.
- Ticket books or stubs—Carnivals, circuses, traveling theater shows, early naturalist supplies including litmus paper and insect tags.
- Others—Die cuts, paper dolls, rewards of merit, road maps.

Pointed Pen Method Roundhand Script

Determine correct slant by using this diagram.
4 up and 3 across.
54° ANGLE.

1 2 3 4 5 ~
5 6 7 8 9 0 ¢ $
1 2 3 4 5 6 7 8 9 0

1.   2.   3.   *Nibs*

Elbow Pen

A B C D E F G H I J K L M
N O P Q R S T U V W X Y Z

abcdefghyklmnopqrstuvwxyzß

Ink Colors

Inkwell

DIDOT typeface c.1810

ABCDEFGHIJKLM
NOPQRSTUVWXYZ
abcdefghijklmnopqrs
tuvwxyz 1234567890

ROMAN italic

ABCDEFGHIJKLM
NOPQRSTUVWXYZ.&c.
abcdefghijklmnopqrstuvw.xyz.
1234567890.

Ink

ENCRE
T.M. PAILLARD
MADE IN FRANCE   NOIRE

Sommeil

The Bedroom

> "Prior to form, prior to color
> or hue, the material must be
> touched. Skin, pillowcase,
> smooth or rough . . .
> prior to the gaze, the grain."
> —*Le Cinq Sens, Michel Serres*

If you decide to use natural fabrics in only one room, the bedroom must be the place. Nothing aids our sleep more than fibrous material that wicks away moisture from our skin, delivering us into a deeper and more restful slumber.

This wisdom was passed on to me one summer from a wonderful older woman at a flea market in Toulouse, France. As I stood there, sweating in the rather cool temperature, she asked if I had trouble sleeping. I told her that I was restless throughout the night and she suggested that I try sleeping under an old hemp sheet, which would regulate my body temperature and allow me to have a calmer night. Sure enough, the following night I slept through and had a peaceful waking.

Since then I have collected early woven natural fiber sheets, and continue to rework them into bedding that is useful in homes today. Mixing these natural fabrics with old French florals, indiennes, tickings, and checks brings a rural feel to the home. Old fabric is precious to me. Somehow I find a way to use every piece, whether it's a patchwork panel hung on the wall or small sachets tucked into drawers. Old cloth carries with it so many secrets; simply touch, smell, and look to appreciate the history of the piece. Even if we can't learn the whole story of a piece of cloth, there are always clues, such as small patches, stains, or repairs that tell us a bit about the previous owner.

INSPIRATIONS

❧ FURNISHING THE ❧ BEDROOM

When it comes to the bedroom, my good friend, Elizabeth Baer, offers this advice:

- Buy the best you can afford—it's better to have too little than second rate.
- Buy in pairs if you get the chance—furniture, ornaments, and pictures. A symmetrical arrangement will always satisfy the eye more than a mix of shapes and sizes, and is sound architecturally.
- Incorporate a touch of red and another of black in every color scheme. It acts as a sort of finishing point for your eye and view, though you may not be aware of it. If you look at a Constable painting, you will see the flash of red on the gate hinges, or elsewhere, and you can use this idea to place a small red lacquered box or decanter stand on a mantelpiece, or a little black snuff box on a table.

BED COVER

A bed cover is a beautiful way to change the look of your bedroom. Start with an old dyed sheet as the base and gather your scraps for a patchwork design.

During the winter months, a bed cover can be made out of an old wool blanket. Make a patchwork cover and button onto the blanket. A button-on cover allows you to use a plain, heavy fabric and add a more decorative panel that can be changed for washing or redecorating.

(See Instructions, page 116.)

Lavendula Spica

LAVENDER BOLSTERS

Along with natural fabrics, lavender is a relaxing herb that ought to be used throughout the home, especially in the bedroom. The minty, medicinal scent is the perfect aroma to assist in relaxing and letting go. Lavender oil applied to your face before retiring to bed aids in falling asleep as well as keeping your skin moisturized.

When introducing lavender to a room, start small; maybe it's just a lavender candle, but then let the scent of lavender permeate throughout the bedroom so that you feel a sense of calm each time you enter. Try spraying lavender water onto your sheets for a fresh scent before you jump into bed.

A comfortable bed is a luxury. Besides sleeping, it's a perfect place for napping or reading. Old French bedrooms had lavender bolsters on their beds. The pillows were used for lounging and the lavender oil was gently released from the seeds whenever one relaxed on the pillow.

To make your own calming resting place, start by making a pillow cover. A king-size pillow makes a nice long lavender bolster. In addition to the pillow cover, make another pillow out of muslin that will attach to the inside of the cover. This inner pillow is the lavender chunnel, a tube of lavender if you will. You need about a pound of lavender to fill a king-size chunnel, less for smaller pillows. The benefit of a chunnel is that you can wash the outer cover without worrying about getting the lavender wet. I like to think that lavender bolsters were used back in the 16th century when there was a need to cover up unwanted smells in the air.

(See Instructions, page 116.)

VINTAGE MILLINERY TIEBACKS

Tiebacks are fabric bands, cords, or other material that shape a curtain or drape and hold it back from the window. Many times you will have extra fabric from an old pair of curtains that you can make into a 4" x 6" band and attach to two small rings, which then attach to a small hook on the wall.

Vintage millinery flowers also make lovely tiebacks. You can use velvet leaves, silk flowers, sap berries, or any other sort of charming botanical shapes. If you can't find a good supply of vintage materials to work with, try a crafts store that stocks new fabric flowers and antique them with a tea dye and a sprinkling of mica dust. This will give the appearance of old flowers stowed in an attic for years.

Enameled flower pins used as tiebacks during the 1920s and '30s are especially useful on lightweight curtains, however, they won't hold the weight of a full-length curtain.

CURTAIN PANELS

Curtain panels from the beginning of the 20th century and earlier were typically quite long in order to accommodate the tall windows in French homes and chateaus. Many of them were never lined, so much of the beautiful old red and pink dyes have faded beyond recognition, however this only adds to the charm and age of these old cloths.

Soon after we bought our home in Los Angeles, Elizabeth Baer sent me a pair of 20-foot-long panels in the most amazing 19th-century red indienne bird print. Indienne fabrics are colorful, cotton florals that were exported to France from India for 400 years.

Luckily, these panels had not been overexposed to light so I lined the panels to stop them from fading while in my care. Lining can be done with either a thick fabric that blocks out all light, or for a softer look, choose summer hemp that will filter out some of the light. Lighter fabric helps panels retain the soft, supple form that allows antique fabric to drape well.

These panels, although quite long, were not wide enough to cover the width of our window. I chose not to alter them, although I could have easily sewn on another panel in a different fabric to make them wider. I always evaluate the piece of antique textile; if it is an important cloth (something that is in very good shape with few flaws), I usually leave it as is.

Curtain hardware is always a challenge. Whether you opt for old or new, consistency is important. With so many wonderful finishes available, you can choose any range of color, from antique gold to oxidized silver, and all sorts of shades in between. I typically prefer working with a warmer, gold-tone finish to give the room a wonderfully aged look.

If you have a lot of windows to cover you may want to try this trick: Use an ordinary copper pipe to make curtain rods. The finials can be rubber balls painted to match. French butcher's hooks (lovely heavy-duty twisted iron) are nice for attaching metal rings to hang curtains from a drapery rod.

HEART SACHETS

I was given a sachet once by an antiques dealer in London in the shape of a heart and it still serves as the prototype for the sachets we make at French General.

I am constantly amazed at the amount of scraps that end up in my workshop. Not wanting to give way to waste, I decided that a lavender sachet was a perfect way to make good use of the beautiful little pieces of fabric found on the cutting floor.

Lavender sachets are quick projects that can be made into almost any shape. If you want to make these without sewing, pick up small muslin bags or old hankies you can fill with dried lavender and tie the ends closed. The thinner or lighter weight fabric you use, the more the essential oil will emanate through the fabric.

Stash sachets in your delicates drawer for the scent or with your wool sweaters to keep moths away. Bundle them with a cutting of old ribbon for a pretty housewarming gift.

(See Instructions, page 117.)

DREAM VESSEL

I always tell my young daughter, Sofia, to think of something she wants to dream about before she falls asleep, which usually sets her on the right track for a calm night. I am not sure this works every night, but we have fun coming up with new stories and ideas.

Molly has thought of another way to keep us inspired and dreaming positive thoughts. A dream vessel is an old jar filled with handwritten or typed inspirations that sits next to the bed. Before going to sleep, simply read one or two of the quotes and try to concentrate on that idea, whether it relates to your work, personal, or creative life. Having this positive image in your mind right before you fall asleep may make it easier to relax.

(See Instructions, page 117.)

BOOKMARKS & BOOKPLATES

The better we treat our books, the longer we will have them in our lives or those lives we've entrusted them to. Bookmarks and bookplates are almost a luxury of the past, but they are an easy way to make a pretty little gift for your books and they use all sorts of old bits you have stuffed in boxes or drawers.

For the bookmark, my sister, Lisa, found an old monogram letter that had been cut off a vintage bed sheet. It had been sewn onto a scrap of fabric similar to an old French banner flag. Punching a hole and attaching a bead, bauble, or tassel onto the end dresses up the bookmark.

Bookplates can be designed out of old labels or tags. Create your own label or photocopy one provided (see Archives, pages 102-113). Attach the label with double-sided adhesive paper or tape and place on the inside cover of your favorite book.

(See Instructions, page 117.)

COVERED JOURNALS

Writing this book has encouraged me to do something I have always resisted—write a little bit every day. This is something our grandparents knew. My grandfather wrote in his journal daily. He wrote about what he wore, the temperature of the day and evening, what he ate, and how many cows he had milked. Mundane thoughts, but they give us a glimpse into what his days were like.

I've always had journals around me to jot down notes, ideas, thoughts, or to plan out goals. I can look back and see the progression of my ideas—simple, complicated, and some even fulfilled. When we started with our product ideas at French General, at the top of our list was a fabric journal cover that could be reused as the pages of each book were filled.

Books can be covered with just about any durable material—old or new. Follow the pattern provided and sew the cover to fit your journal or consider using some of the bookbinding techniques from the guest book.

(See Instructions, page 118.)

PAPERWEIGHTS

Decorative novelties such as the paperweight first appeared during the 1840s. For the next 25 years, the three great French glasshouses of Saint Louis, Clichy, and Baccarat competed with each other in the manufacture of the most beautiful and functional paperweights. With the popularity of letter writing, paperweights became a collectible item as well as a much-traded and collected piece.

Keep a lookout for vintage paperweight blanks at antique stores or markets. Lay a treasured photograph or piece of fabric underneath the glass weight. If you use a crystal dome-shaped paperweight, you will see a magnifying effect.

Try decoupaging underneath the glass with a favorite image or maybe even a small button card or photograph. Almost anything relatively flat will work. My mom used some cuttings of old cross-stitch monograms and fabric scraps to make her own unique collection of paperweights.

JEWELRY BOX

If you are a jewelry collector, you know that collecting small jewelry boxes or baskets is just as important as the gems you hold on to. I try to keep my collections of jewels and baubles organized according to color, but many times they end up organized according to type of jewelry: silver bracelets in one box, small rings in another, and long necklaces hanging from old hooks on the back of a door.

Perhaps you may want to collect small celluloid boxes for your earrings and rings. We usually see loads of these at the flea markets in England and they are in surprisingly great shape, some more than 150 years old.

You also can build a jewelry box for your dresser out of wood or cardboard. My husband built this box for me using cardboard and decorative paper. Add a touch of detail to your handmade boxes by gluing on vintage nail-head glass beads, cabochons, or sequins.

(See Instructions, page 118.)

Add a touch of detail to your handmade boxes by gluing on vintage nail-head glass beads, cabochons, or sequins.

WALL HANGINGS

Years ago I came across a basement filled with vintage fabrics in New York at a shop called Aix. There were shelves filled to the ceiling, lined with old document French florals, tickings, and quilts. I started to buy into this collection, slowly at first, and then with every penny I could spare. Some pieces were no bigger than a 20" x 20" document scrap, but it didn't matter to me. What I had found were pieces of history, and I set out to preserve some of these rare French fabrics.

Since many of these pieces were too delicate to make anything that would be useful, I made a series of wall hangings with medieval tapestries in mind. I lined the back of the fabric with a soft hemp textile and then sewed a pocket at the top for a rod to fit through. At the end of each rod I attached drawer pulls for the finials. An old piece of chain or ribbon completes the tapestry or wall hanging. This is a great project to make with a piece of antique fabric that might have a hole here or there.

Although purely decorative—and not particularly useful for its original purpose of keeping old stone walls warm— these wall hangings can warm the look of a room by adding color and texture to the walls.

XIX siècle . Tissus

34-36 motif exotique . bambou . des oiseaux

37-40 florales imprimées

41-45 toiles à matelas

46-49 motif indienne

50-52 kelsch . carreaux

LAVOIR

CHAPTER

4

The Laundry Room

"We should all do what, in
the long run, gives us joy,
even if it is only picking
grapes or sorting the laundry."
—E.B. White

Growing up, our laundry room was visited as often as the kitchen. My mom washed clothes for seven of us on a daily basis. I always wished our laundry room was decorated—or had more of a personality, like the rest of our home—so we could be comfortable while folding clothes or looking for that lost sock.

Even today, when I go home, I am surprised to find clothes soaking and the dryer running pretty regularly, although now more often than not it's the sheets we have brought back from France that my mom restores to their original condition.

More than 100 years old, these hemp, nettle, and linen sheets are in remarkable shape once they have been spotted, soaked, washed, and laid outside on the grass to dry in the sun.

The washing room was an important room in the French house. This developed after the upper class could afford to have rooms built especially for this purpose. Decades earlier, the communal lavoires were the only place to air your dirty laundry. A lavoire was an old stone fountain that was used for washing household textiles and clothes.

Although a romantic notion, you may want to rethink this idea of the laundry room as being only a room for household chores. Make your "laundry" space an enjoyable area where you'll want to go to do more than just cleaning.

Laundry rooms can be great storage rooms. With extra baskets and shelves, you can store much more than just clothing waiting to be ironed. Consider beautiful ways to contain and display your home cleaning products, baskets of cleaning cloths, and old project supplies.

INSPIRATIONS

❧ TEA STAINING TIPS ❧

Natural fabrics such as cotton, linen, hemp, or nettle work best for dyeing as they absorb the color or dye more evenly. Be sure to wash the fabric to be dyed first to address any shrinking issues.

To begin, boil 4 quarts of water, and then add 2-4 tea bags, depending on how dark you want the fabric. Let the tea bags steep for as long as necessary (up to 5 minutes). Experiment with different types of tea bags to obtain a variety of colors. Try chamomile for a subtle mellow yellow, or a cranberry tea for a burnt red color.

Before you add the fabric to your tea mixture, soak it until it is completely wet. Squeeze out excess water, place the fabric in the tea water, and then gently stir. Let the fabric sit until the desired color is achieved. Remember, the dye will appear darker when it is wet. Remove the fabric and rinse well in the sink with a little dishwashing liquid. Hang line to dry.

LAUNDRY BASKET LINER

Large baskets are great for piling clean sheets in the laundry room. You can usually find big baskets at country flea markets, or make a dash for the garage at the next estate sale and maybe you'll find a collection.

We hit upon a good supply of old laundry baskets through a French importer. The different sizes and shapes of baskets inspired us to sew a liner into each of them and use them to sort darks, whites, and reds.

LAUNDRY BAG

Rather than think of a laundry bag as a place to put dirty clothes, consider it a useful storage bag for wool sweaters, extra pillows, or bedding.

An old French grain bag woven out of hemp inspired this bag. If you use cotton muslin, think about tea staining it to get the look of an old farm bag. To authenticate it, stencil a word or phrase in French like "Il faut laver son linge sale en famille," roughly translated into "Don't air your dirty laundry in public," or consider "Demain il fera jour," which means "Tomorrow is another day." My favorite French saying is "Elle se sent bonne dans sa peau," or "She feels good in her skin."

(See Instructions, page 119.)

HANGER COVERS

Covered hangers are a small luxury. No one really needs them, but they certainly spruce up wire hangers and are befitting a special dress or crisp shirt.

Making hanger covers, which included padded hangers, was popular in the 1940s and '50s. The covers can be knitted, crocheted, or sewn from fabric. We've sewn a set of covers using a linen mangle cloth. These cloths were used at the turn of the last century on mangle presses to protect the clean linen from the rollers used to press large linen sheets, drapes, and tablecloths.

The beauty of using a fibrous cloth as a hanger cover is that you can hang something wet and the linen will absorb the moisture, speeding up the drying process. Many people throw away their wire hangers from the cleaners; making fabric covers is a great way to recycle and reuse an otherwise unwanted household object. You can also look for sets of covered hangers at estate sales. Head straight for the master bedroom closet—it may be filled with all sorts of styles.

(See Instructions, page 119.)

CLOTHESPIN BAGS

Clothespins, although not used as much as they once were, are still useful around the house and in the garden. Use clothespins to hold vines to trellises or to attach labels to potted plants, to make a quick child's bib by clipping a dishcloth to their shirt, to use as a note holder, to hold songbooks open, or, my personal favorite, to keep a bag of chips closed.

A clothespin bag can be made with fabric scraps and a child's hanger. Hang the bag outside near your clothesline or in your laundry room for easy access. Using stronger materials will allow laundry bags to survive the outside elements.

(See Instructions, page 120.)

BLANCHEUR,
SOUPLESSE & FINESSE

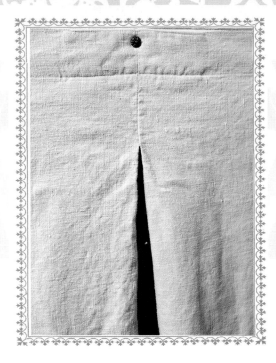

SINK SKIRT

Originally used in French washrooms, the sink skirt was made
out of heavy woven hemp and used to cover up washboards,
soaps, and cleaning materials. To recreate this look and give
your laundry room a rural French feel, design a skirt to attach
to your sink. This will soften the look of a washroom as well
as serve a functional purpose.

Look for an old monogrammed sheet with your initials
on it or have yours embroidered onto a piece of drop cloth
readily available at most home improvement stores and then
use this as the fabric for your skirt. By adding this small piece
you will personalize your laundry room and make it into your
own workspace.

A sink skirt with or without pleats can be sewn from a
heavy hemp or linen fabric that will wear well. If you are
planning to attach the skirt underneath the sink, use hook-
and-loop tape or sew small buttonholes to the skirt and attach
it to hooks on the inside of the sink. If the frame is made out
of wood, simply attach the skirt with upholstery tacks.

(See Instructions, page 120.)

FLOOR CLOTH

Since the 1800s, floor cloths have been a presence in French homes. Originally used to cover the natural floors and to keep rooms warm, they were woven out of rustic hemp fibers and withstood many years of use. Using a floor cloth in your laundry room between the washer and the dryer can absorb extra moisture and protect clothes that may fall on the floor.

My mom made this floor cloth with a piece of heavy muslin that she painted with a border, then coated with several layers of varnish to give it a high sheen and to make it water resistant.

Get inspiration for borders from old soap labels, candy wrappers, or tin cans. The border on our floor cloth was inspired by the French General logo.

AIR FRESHENERS

Nothing is worse than a laundry room that smells like bleach or other toxic cleaning agents. To naturally freshen the air, hang dried lavender around your utility room, or make up several lavender wands and tuck them into drawers or hang them from hangers. Lavender is also a great moth repellent placed in linen bags and armoires to ward off evil pests.

Another great way to keep your rooms and linens smelling fresh is linen water. The French use linen water to iron their sheets, spraying again just before laying a duvet over bed sheets. Linen water can be made using any essential oil: lavender, sage, linden, rose, hydrangea, orange blossom, or by combining oils to come up with your own scent.

INSPIRATIONS

❧ LAVENDER LINEN WATER ❧

Ingredients

1 tsp. (100 drops) lavender essential oil

2 oz. denatured alcohol

10 oz. distilled water

12 oz. bottle with lid

Instructions

Pour essential oil and alcohol into bottle, close lid or cap, and shake to mix; add distilled water. Mixture will become cloudy and eventually separate. Shake well before each use.

lavage avec le détergent de
LAVANDE

POWDERED LAUNDRY SOAP

Developing our own laundry soap for 200-year-old fabric was a great challenge for us. We needed a detergent that was strong enough to remove old stains but still gentle enough to protect old fibers. Our laundry soap is scented with lavender oil, but you can choose any essential oil.

Simply combine 1 cup grated heavy-duty laundry soap bar, ½ cup washing soda, ½ cup borax, and 2 tsp. essential oil. Makes enough for 8-10 loads of laundry.

An easy way to store laundry soap in a fun way is to decoupage a French-themed label on a metal bucket, sew a liner for the inside of the bucket, then tuck in your plastic bag filled with laundry soap. A ribbon can be tied around the top of the liner for a pretty finishing touch.

a.

PORTE - HABITS PARIS

b.

AU PRINTEMPS

c.

MASCOTTE

a. Glycérine

b. Sèl fin

c. HYDROGÈNE PEROXYDE

d. alcool

e. Vinaigre

a. b. c. d. e. f. g.

h. i. j. k. l. m.

Pinces à Linge

Sac pour les Pinces

SAVON LAVANDE

Blanchaye Souplesse et Finesse

200 ml.

100 ml.

citrons

32
24
16
8

f. PERRIER eau minérale

Seau

Panier

Planche à Repasser

JARDIN DES VARIÉTÉS

The Garden

I didn't understand what a garden could be until I worked in my own yard. Our first home—in Grandview, New York, along the Hudson River—was on almost an acre of land. When spring arrived, I decided to try planting a garden to see if I could create something that would last through the seasons. To my surprise I not only arranged and planted a small garden, I was able to tend it throughout the winter and the perennials returned as full as ever the following spring.

With the help of a neighbor, whose calling card read "Just Ask," I learned how to plant, prune, and deadhead—tasks that ensure a healthy season. I now work with Anselmo, a gardener whose ancestors have worked the fields in California for the past 100 years, migrating north during the summer for the strawberry season and heading south to pick oranges in the winter. Whether he's helping me plant my vegetable garden or propagating roses, Anselmo has taught me that even a small garden needs constant care and patience.

The garden has always been one of the calmest places for me. I bring a bit of the inside out by layering ticking pillows on benches and setting up old iron tables and chairs. Throughout warmer months, the garden serves as another room of our home.

Whether you have a small patch of land in the backyard or potted herbs on the kitchen shelf, the garden is a great inspiration to those who see the natural design in every leaf, bud, and petal.

FABRICATION
FRANÇAISE
MARQUE DÉP

INSPIRATIONS

&❧ CITRUS FOOT SCRUB ❧&

Ingredients

½ - 1 tsp. fresh lemon juice

1 cup sea salt

1 Tbs. almond oil

1 Tbs. avocado oil

1 Tbs. vitamin E oil

6 drops Neroli oil (or lavender)

Instructions

Blend all ingredients together in a mortar and pestle (if you use a finer salt it will be easier). Store in a sealed tight jar, preferably dark, to protect the essential oil. If you are not going to use the scrub within a day or two, store mixture in the refrigerator. Scoop out a handful of salt oil and brush on with a small foot brush to keep your feet smooth.

LAVENDER POTIONS & SALTS

Lavender is well known for its unique fragrance. Its name is derived from the Latin word lavare, or, "to wash." It was used throughout Europe during the 17th century to disguise unsavory household odors and textiles that were only washed twice a year. The Greeks and Romans used it in their bath water, while years later ladies of refinement carried lavender sprigs tucked in their tussie mussies. Lavender has also been used medicinally for hundreds of years.

Today lavender can be applied to treat sunburns and minor cuts and scrapes. Cool compresses soaked in strong lavender tea promote healing for sunburns as well as other minor skin problems. It is also known to counter insomnia and promote restful sleep. A lavender-mint tea, for example, calms the senses and helps you relax. Place a few drops of essential oil on the cooled light bulbs in your lamps. When you turn on the lamps, the heat from the bulbs will warm the oil and disperse its scent throughout the room.

Lavender is a hardy, low-maintenance plant that grows quite easily on a hill or in a backyard with good soil and drainage. I have some plants that have grown to be more than 4 feet wide. You can also buy lavender in bulk from dried herb suppliers or by the scoopful at most health food stores.

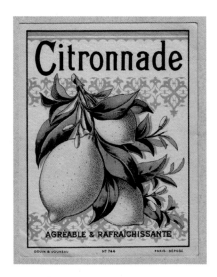

INSPIRATIONS

❧ GRASSE BATH SALTS ❧

Ingredients

½ cup baking soda

½ cup epsom salts

½ cup fresh lavender, sage, rosemary

½ cup sea salt

5 drops lavender essential oil

Instructions

Blend the above ingredients in a food processor or blender. (You can substitute the essential oil for another, for example, geranium, orange blossom, or rose.) Place ½ cup of blended salts in a cotton muslin bag and run under warm water when filling your tub. You can also let your feet soak in the salts once the salts dissolve a bit. The salts actually drain the aches from your muscles, while the soothing scents fill you with a sense of calm and well being.

INSPIRATIONS

❧ PICKING AND DRYING ❧ LAVENDER

Lavender is used in the home for its sweet scent. To preserve your own lavender, gather the plant for drying when the first bud on the flower stalk is starting to open. Some varieties, such as Hidcote, remain tightly closed for some time, which allows you 7–10 days to do your harvesting. Other species, like Croxton Wild, are completely open in a day or two, which often causes them to lose their blossoms in the drying process.

Be sure to cut your lavender stems just after the dew is off of them early in the morning. If you wait until later in the day, the plant will have lost its essential oil in the process of cooling down.

To dry lavender, bind 25–75 stems with a rubber band and hang in a warm, dry, dark spot for 4-5 weeks. When completely dry, store in cardboard boxes or cloth bags.

INSPIRATIONS

❧ HERBAL BATH BAGS ❧

Ingredients

½ cup dried rosemary

1 cup dried lavender flowers

1 cup dried lemon balm

1 cup dried mint

1 cup dried rose petals

Instructions

Blend the above ingredients in a food processor
or blender or crush finely with a mortar and pestle.
Fill small cotton muslin bags and tie drawstring
tightly. Let bags steep in a hot bath—the water
will be infused with the scent of a fresh garden.

HERBAL POTS & MARKERS

Growing an herb garden is more of a garden activity than a craft, though there are ways to embellish your containers so they become a decorative part of your home. Start with small terra-cotta pots and paint or whitewash them with an acrylic paint.

Add an aged look to unsealed terra-cotta pots by growing moss on them. Simply place a large cup full of moss and ¼ cup of water in a blender and grind until crumbly. Coat the pots with plain, soured yogurt and then rub with the moss mixture. Set treated pots in a cool, damp, shaded area for a couple of weeks and mist them daily.

You can bring these small pots into the house, so consider planting herbs you might like to cook with, such as basil, sage, or rosemary. Once you've planted with potting soil, mark the pots with a permanent marker, either directly on the pot or on plant markers. Keep your eye out for old plant markers at antique shops and flea markets, which can usually be re-painted and used over and over.

At Brimfield one year, my sister and I found a couple hundred metal plant markers. The die-cut metal markers came from a 1920s botanical shop in Connecticut. Each one had such a romantic plant name, like Kiss Me Over the Garden Gate, Yesterday, Today, and Tomorrow, Love Lies Bleeding, and Love in a Mist. Many customers in our New York store dug through them and found their favorite plant names.

We discovered great reproductions of these markers, painted them with an antique wash of color, and then wrote the names of plants on them with a permanent marker.

INSPIRATIONS

❧ HERBS DE PROVENCE ❧ MIXTURE

There are many different varieties of this wonderful dried herb blend. The following recipe was given to me by a dealer at the St. Antonin farmer's market, held every Sunday morning in the medieval village of St. Antonin de Noble Val, just an hour north of Toulouse, France. Using Herbs de Provence is a great way to cook with the sweet herb of lavender.

Ingredients

2 Tbs. lavender flowers

3 Tbs. oregano leaves

3 Tbs. savory leaves

3 Tbs. thyme leaves

1 tsp. basil leaves

1 tsp. rosemary leaves

1 tsp. sage leaves

Instructions

Combine and mix well. Store mixture in a small airtight jar in a cool, dark location. Makes about ¾ cup. Use for salad dressings and as a poultry, beef, or fish rub.

ÉTAGÈRE

Étagère is a French term for a piece of furniture with open, decorative shelves for displaying small objects. Keeping potted herbs in the garden was our inspiration for turning these wooden milk crates into an étagère.

To create your own étagère, start with a few boxes or crates, found at tag sales, estate sales, or local craft shops. Sand down any paint or varnish, then choose an organic color that will fit into your garden space—verdigris, madder, indigo, or ochre, for example.

After painting, let boxes dry overnight. Meanwhile, find a print reminiscent of 19th-century French seed packets or agriculture company logos, or stencil French wording onto the crates. Adhere printed images onto the sides of the crates with decoupage medium and let dry. If you desire, use fine-grit sandpaper to gently distress the edges to give it an aged appearance.

(See Instructions, page 120.)

LEAF PRESSING & HERBIER

An herbier is essentially what we call an herbarium specimen—a dried, pressed plant attached to a sheet of paper identified with the plant's Latin name, family, location, and date it was collected. An herbarium specimen is the time-honored way of identifying plants and serves as a means of studying and classifying them.

Traditionally, herbiers are made with only one plant to a page. However, some naturalists historically have made herbiers with collections of specimens from a particular locale or habitat. An offshoot of this practice was the Victorian pastime of making keepsake herbiers, with a selection of plants organized to serve as a reminder of a certain garden or voyage.

Many people in France make their own herbiers as a means of learning about plants and memorizing their identifications. Once you begin to prepare herbier pages, you will become intimately acquainted with the plant's characteristics.

Collect your plants in the early morning just after the dew has dried and then arrange the fresh flowers or leaves between sheets of blotting paper. You can make your own flower press with a few layers of chipboard tightly closed with ribbons. After a couple of days, open and check your plants. Continue to dry, allowing your specimens to dry completely (about 1-3 weeks).

After your specimen has completely dried, it's time to affix it to a page. Choose a quality, moderately absorbent thick paper such as watercolor stock. Arrange your plant specimen on the page and fix it firmly in place with narrow strips of paper tape. Using your finest script, label the sheet with all of the appropriate information.

If you display your herbier prints, be sure to place them out of direct light to minimize the fading of colors. Also be sure to date your herbier. The mysterious attraction of the herbier lies in its ability to preserve the fragility of a flower for countless decades—a simple bit of magic that modern times have not improved on.

(See Instructions, page 121.)

HERB CARDS

Another fun way to preserve your cuttings is to adhere them to cards made with cardstock or another type of thick paper. Place your dried specimen on the card, tape in place, and write its name under the herb. For fun, and to practice your language skills, you may want to write the name in Latin or French.

Store your cards in an old wooden or cardboard box painted and embellished with botanical drawings. Photocopy your favorite vintage label or one we've provided (see Archives, pages 102–113) and adhere to the top of the box with craft glue or decoupage medium.

(See Instructions, page 121.)

PLEIN AIR STOOLS

Plein air is a French term meaning "in the open air." Artist Claude Monet was the quintessential plein air painter. He was fixated on capturing the effects of light on the landscape in a nearly scientific way, and capturing the atmospheric "envelope" of the landscape. One can imagine that Monet enjoyed many summer days sitting on a small stool overlooking the "light" near his home in Giverny, France in the 1800s.

Monet's preoccupation with reducing all visual experience to terms of pure light became an obsession. When his young wife died he was horrified to find himself analyzing the nacreous tints of her skin in the early morning light. As he continued to paint, wishing he could have been "born blind in order to gain his sight and be able to paint objects without knowing what they were," he began more and more to develop the ability to see light and nothing but light; light became like a corrosive substance eating away the objects bathed in it.

One summer, while my family and I were driving through Provence, I suddenly saw "the light." From then on we have referred to a certain time of day when one can actually see the reflection of the light change the landscape. The garden is the perfect place to see the light change, if you are patient enough to wait for it.

To help you wait for the light, fill your garden with small stools that are easy to move around. The wooden bases of these stools were found in a hardware shop in Paris, but you can find similar ones in camping supply stores. I cut pieces of old ticking and wrapped the ends around the stool frames, then attached them under each side using decorative upholstery tacks. By making ticking covers for the seats, the stools feel as if they are right out of a garden in southern France.

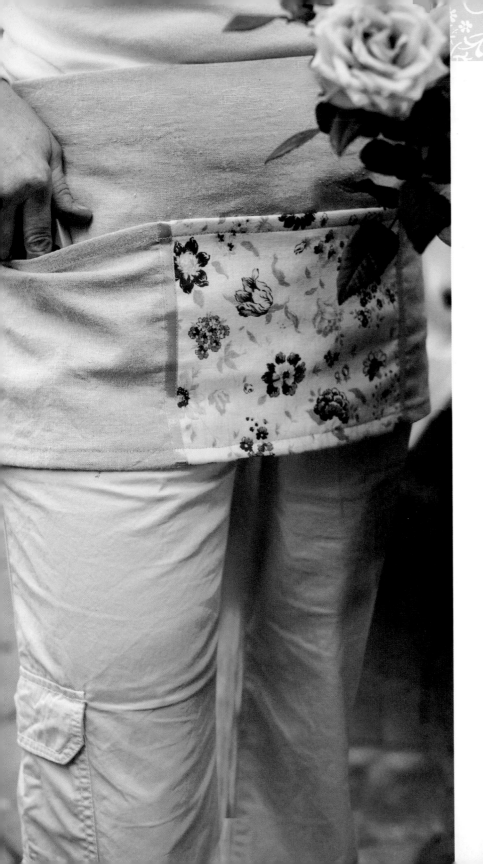

GARDEN APRON

I am a big believer in aprons, whether they're worn in the kitchen or garden. Aprons have traditionally been seen on men who labored in the trades: butchers, bakers, and blacksmiths. In this context, we think of aprons as symbols of honest, hard, and important work. I love this definition of the apron. It makes me feel that when wearing my apron I will work hard, or at least do hard work.

Our apron project is a simple sewing craft that uses a pattern and natural hemp material. We chose to use hemp for its natural strength, and no matter how much dirt you grind into it, hemp retains its beauty, wash after wash.

When making this project, feel free to alter the pattern to suit your own needs. Perhaps you are looking for an apron that will cover more of your legs, or more of your sides to wipe your hands. Our garden apron is ideal for working in the garden as it is short enough to not hinder your work while kneeling on the ground. It also has enough pockets to tuck in garden tools, gloves, and seed packets. You can alter our pattern to create a butcher-style apron—a long ankle-length piece perfect for wearing in the kitchen.

(See Instructions, page 121.)

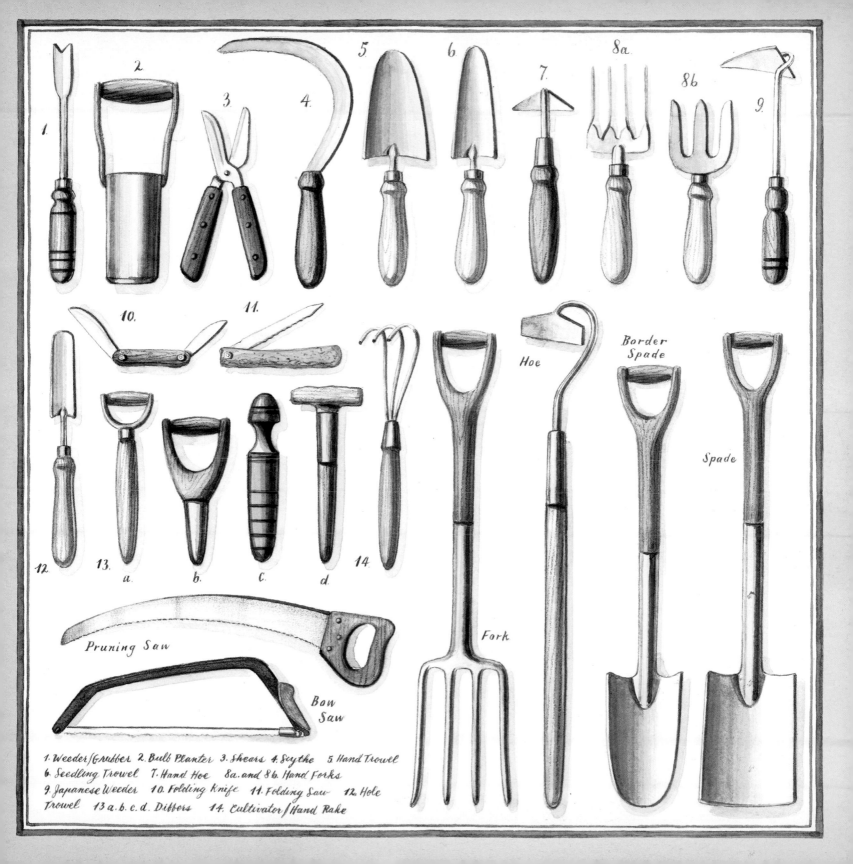

Pruning Saw

Bow Saw

Hoe

Border Spade

Spade

Fork

1. Weeder / Grubber   2. Bulb Planter   3. Shears   4. Scythe   5. Hand Trowel
6. Seedling Trowel   7. Hand Hoe   8a. and 8b. Hand Forks
9. Japanese Weeder   10. Folding Knife   11. Folding Saw   12. Hole
Trowel   13 a. b. c. d. Dibbers   14. Cultivator / Hand Rake

GENTIANE

Type

Date

Use

N°

MIXTURE

N°

LONDON

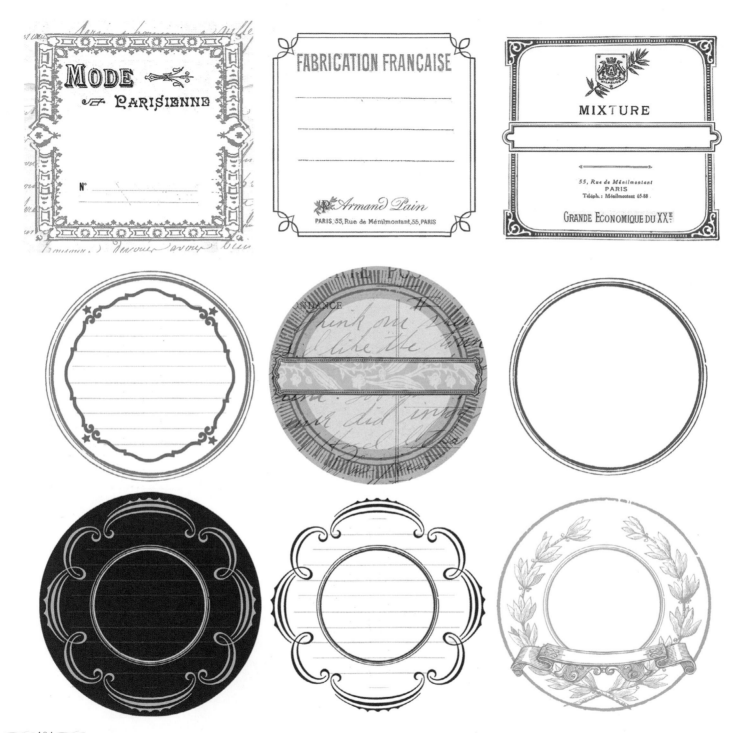

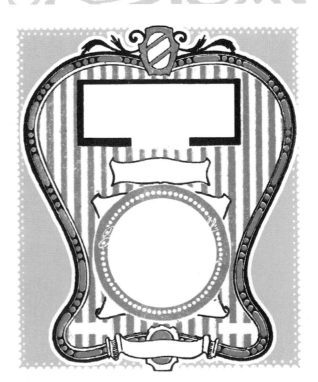

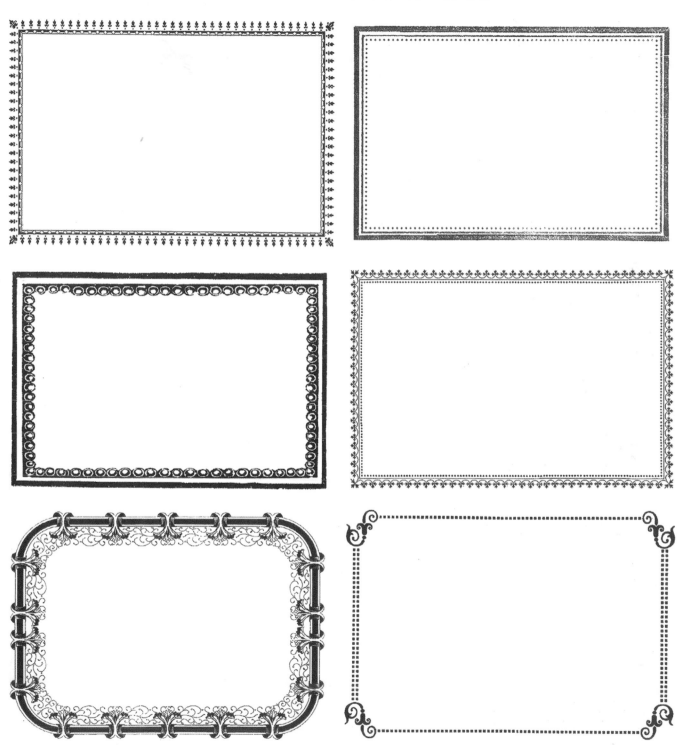

ABCDEFGHIJKLMNOPQRST
UVWXYZ!?()1234567890⚜

ABCDEFGHIJKLMNO
PQRSTUVWXYZ&#!()

abcdefghijklmnopqrst
uvwxyz 1234567890

huile d'olive vinaigre
vin rouge léau de toile
biscuits jardin bonheur
menthe limon orange
lait souvenir fleur

POSTCARD GARLAND

(Pages 34-35)

Materials

- Decorative scissors
- Old notions: beads, buttons, cabochons, sequins, glitter
- Ribbon
- Dresdens
- Hole punch
- Postcards: old and new

Instructions

To make the garland, punch a hole in top corners of each card. Glue on decorative bits and pieces that complement the image. Try old dresdens around the edges, glitter to outline flower petals and leaves, and buttons sewn on to look like an old button card. Thread ribbon through holes and tie ends into a bow.

INSPIRATION BOARD

(Page 39)

Materials

- ¼"-thick plywood
- ⅛"-thick foam
- Brown kraft paper
- Cardboard: 2 sheets
- Electric nail gun
- Picture hanger hooks
- Ribbon: 2 yards
- Table saw
- ⅛"-thick chipboard
- 18" x 18" fabric
- Buttons
- Craft glue
- Hammer
- Pliers
- Scissors

Instructions

Cut chipboard to 14" x 14" with table saw. Cut plywood into four ¾" x 14" strips. Place strips underneath chipboard, flush with edges (A). **Note:** The ends of the strip will stick out from the corners.

Staple nails into chipboard and strips around each side. Trim corners with diagonal cut using table saw. Cut 14¼" x 14¼" of foam, glue inside edges of flat chipboard, and place foam on top. Place 18" x 18" fabric face down and chipboard on top with foam side facing down centered. Pull each side of fabric edge over and around plywood and staple one nail for each side (B). Stretch fabric as you do this.

Turn board over. Cut four 18" lengths of ribbon and place each one about 3" in from each side. Staple first ribbon overlap. Work your way around, stapling other three overlaps while firmly pulling taut each ribbon. Make sure ribbons are kept straight and even.

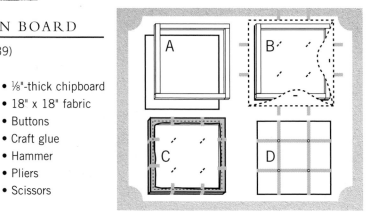

Flip board over and bend down staples that came through with pliers. Staple edges of fabric and ribbon onto plywood all the way around (C). Make sure to pull fabric firmly.

Cut cardboard to fit back side of memory board. Cut 13¼" x 13¼" kraft brown paper; glue edges and place down; wipe off any excess glue. Trim corners diagonally to match those of board.

Attach picture hanger hook on back side. Glue buttons to front side of board where ribbons overlap (D). Allow glue to bond (2-3 hours) before hanging inspiration board.

TEXTILES FOR THE TABLE

(Pages 50-51)

Note: Some sewing experience is needed with a sewing machine. If your experience is limited, try sewing some of the simple projects first. Use sharp scissors for cutting on a clean, flat area. Hem by folding ½" over and then fold another ½". All fabric should be washed and pressed first. If hemmed edges will not flatten with pressing, wash and dry them; they should flatten once pressed again.

Materials

- Fabric
- Ribbon or trim
- Sewing machine
- Iron and ironing board
- Sewing scissors

Instructions

To make napkins: Cut fabric to 14" x 9". Hem all sides. Press. Sew on ribbon or trim in desired pattern or add monogram to front of napkin (center-front placement is preferable).

To make place mats: Cut fabric to 18" x 18" or 20" x 20". Sew down ribbon or trim 4" in from edges. Hem all sides. Press.

To make table runner: Cut fabric width and length of choice—runner should hang about 12" off either end of the table and be about 12"-18" wide. Hem all sides. Press.

ETCHED GLASSES

(Pages 52-53)

Materials

• Drinking glasses	• Etching cream
• Paintbrush: small	• Pencil (optional)
• Rubber cement	• Scissors
• Stencils: small	• Towel

Instructions

After cleaning and drying glasses, position stencil on outside surface. Flexible, self-sticking stencils available at crafts stores are easiest to use, or you can cut your own from the template provided (see Archives, pages 102-113). Copy on a thick but flexible piece of plastic or self-adhesive acetate, found in art supply stores, and tack down lightly with rubber cement. **Note:** The stencil must lie flat, free of any air bubbles, to get a clean image.

Paint on a thick layer of etching cream with a small brush, enough to cover entire area. You can also create polka dots by sticking a pencil eraser into etching cream and dotting on glass.

You can also use stamps or use the brush only. Let piece sit at least 5 minutes, and then wash and dry with towel.

GUEST BOOK

(Page 54)

Materials

• 8½" x 11" text-weight paper (20-50 sheets, depending on desired thickness of book, paper can be torn on edges for a more vintage look)

• Binder clips	• Bone folder
• Book board (⅛" thick)	• Book cloth
• Brush	• Decorative paper
• Exacto knife	• Hand drill or awl
• Pencil	• PVA glue
• Ribbon	• Ruler
• Scissors	

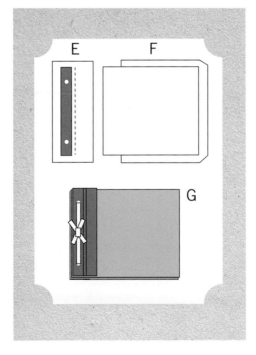

Instructions

To prepare covers: Cut book board for spine measuring 1" x 8¾". Mark vertical centerline on spine piece ½" from top edge and another mark ½" up from bottom edge (E). Evenly space three more marks along centerline between those two marks. Drill or punch holes on spine where you have made pencil marks. Cut book cloth measuring 4" x 10¾". Glue spine board onto book cloth, leaving 1" of book cloth on left side, top, and bottom (there should be 2" on right side of spine). Flip over and carefully press book cloth with bone folder to remove any air bubbles. Flip back over and draw vertical line on book cloth ⅜" from right edge of spine. Cut book board for cover measuring 9¾" x 8¾". Glue book board cover along line drawn on book cloth (F). (This will create the gutter, allowing book to open and close.) Fold and glue book cloth corners at top, bottom, and left edges of book board. Cut decorative paper 10¾" x 10", leaving 1" extra on three sides of book board cover. Glue decorative paper to book board cover, overlapping book cloth by ¼". Fold in and glue corners, top, and bottom of decorative paper on inside book board cover. Cover inside of book board cover with decorative paper or book cloth. Repeat for second cover.

To prepare text block: Stack pages (20 to 50 sheets) and clip together with binder clips lengthwise. Mark binding holes as you did with spine, ½" from left edge of page. Create holes for binding with drill or awl. These holes will line up with holes you made in spine.

To assemble book: Place text block between two covers and secure entire book with binder clips. Weave ribbon through holes in bootlace fashion and tie in a bow or square knot (G).

MENU CARDS & PLACE CARDS

(Pages 56-58)

Materials

- Baker's string
- Craft glue
- Fine-point pen: black
- Notions: assorted
- Ribbon
- Stamps
- Scissors
- Small beads
- Cardstock or cardboard
- Inkpad and rubber stamps
- Ribbon: herringbone
- Stencils
- String

Instructions

To make menu card: Copy the template provided (see Archives, pages 102-113) onto heavy cardstock or cardboard; cut out two matching pieces. On backside, glue down ½" x 3½" piece of herringbone or woven cotton ribbon (ribbon serves as spine attachment that will hold cards together). Once you have tent shape and glue has dried, decorate menu card with old label, ribbon, and/or stamps. **Note:** You can make smaller cards and place at each setting or one fabulous card for the table.

To make place cards: Place cards are done much the same way using a smaller card. After copying template, cut out two sides and glue ribbon inside to hold together. Decorate with notions and write out name of each guest or use small alphabet stamps. We've included a bird stencil (see Archives, pages 102-113). Once you cut out bird place card, cut out an additional smaller tag, which the name is written on, and sew on short piece of baker's string and glue to beak.

BED COVER

(Page 62)

Materials

- Fabric (for base)
- Measuring tape
- Safety pins
- Scrap fabric
- Sewing machine
- Sewing scissors

Instructions

Note: The final design will depend on your fabrics and layout. Start with a solid base—this can be a blanket or a sheet, or use heavy fabric, like hemp, and make your own. We dyed our base a coral red and then laid out all sorts of old pink and red florals and tickings. Follow these guidelines for general bed cover sizes: twin 68" x 86"; full 80" x 90"; queen 86" x 94"; king 110" x 96".

Once you have base sewn with 1" hem to one of the above sizes, you are ready to start patchwork. With scraps, design your own template on top of base fabric. Lay out rectangles and add small squares and stripes. Move pieces around until you find right balance. Once you find what you like, pin pieces onto base with safety pin (you need ½" on all sides for seam allowance).

Keep these loosely attached so you can sew around them but they will still remain in place. Start sewing bottom pieces on first and work your way up. This may require some careful measurements if you want a balance of pieces all around.

LAVENDER BOLSTERS

(Page 63)

Materials

- Dried lavender
- Fabric: decorative, such as brocade, to cover front of pillow
- Hot glue gun
- Needle and thread
- Pillow: thin cotton to hold lavender
- Sewing machine
- Sewing scissors
- Trim: enough for all edges of fabric

Instructions

Note: This project can be made with any size pillow. In this project a king-size pillow was used.

Cut two pieces of fabric size needed to make envelope slightly shorter than height of pillow and same width as pillow. Sew three sides and three channels of the fabric together with sewing machine (A). Fill pockets with dried lavender (B). Sew fourth side of envelope closed by hand. Attach fabric envelope to pillow using hot glue gun on corners and edges. Insert pillow and lavender filled pockets in to a pillow cover.

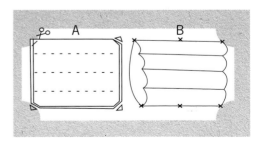

PILLOWS

(Page 63)

Materials
- Fabric: assorted coordinating colors, patterns
- Measurement tape
- Pillows
- Ribbon ties (optional)
- Sewing machine
- Sewing scissors
- Zipper (optional)

Instructions

Note: This project is a lot like the bed cover—you get to use up all your old scraps and make small picture pillows. You can stick to the same color scheme as the bed cover and use the same color base for the back of the pillows. Again, play with the layout. Try different sizes on each pillow.

To make pillow cover, measure pillow and cut fabric with 1" seam allowance. Before sewing pillow together, sew on scraps to top of front using same techniques as above. Turn front and back piece on wrong side and sew up all three sides (C). You can either make closure with ribbon ties (D) or add zipper. Turn right side out and stuff with pillow.

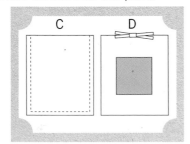

HEART SACHETS

(Page 66-67)

Materials
- Dried lavender: 1 cup
- Fabric: 14" x 14"
- Funnel or paper rolled to make a cone
- Heart template
- Iron and ironing board
- Needle and thread
- Sewing scissors

Instructions

Cut out hearts and stitch together with ½" seam allowance (E). Leave 2" open along side for lavender. Cut "V" shapes out of seam allowances around curves (F). Clip into seam allowance at inner point as close and carefully as possible. Trim down outer point as well. Turn right side out and press. Fill with lavender to desired fullness (G). Hand stitch opening closed with small stitches (H); triple stitch this to prevent it from opening.

DREAM VESSEL

(Page 67)

Materials
- Apothecary or jam jar
- Decorative-edge scissors
- Old ledger paper
- Old typewriter
- Pencil

Instructions

With an old typewriter, print inspirational lines and quotes on old ledger or tea-stained paper. Cut sayings into strips with decorative-edge scissors and then wrap each one around a pencil to curl the strip. You may want to cut ends in "V" shape like an old piece of ribbon. Drop strips into old jar and read one a day. After reading keep pressed in a book or spike onto an old receipt poker.

BOOKMARKS

(Page 68)

Materials
- Cardboard
- Decorative ribbon or tassel
- Embroidered monogram
- Fabric glue
- Hole punch (optional)
- Notions: assorted

- Old fabric or felt
- Scissors
- String or tassel (optional)

Instructions

Cut out desired shape of bookmark from cardboard. Cut out fabric to completely cover cardboard. Glue fabric to cardboard; let dry. Sew or glue notions onto cardboard. If desired, punch hole at top and tie on string or tassel with large bead that can hang from tassel.

COVERED JOURNALS

(Page 69)

Materials

- Blank journal or book
- Fabric
- Fabric marker
- Interfacing
- Iron
- Measuring tape
- Sewing scissors
- Straight pins

Instructions

Measure journal. (The best way to do this is with a measuring tape or the fabric itself.) Insert tape or fabric into open cover of journal, allowing at least 3" to cover inside. Close cover on it and wrap tape or fabric around rest of book. Mark measurement at center of spine, then double that and add 1"—this is your width measurement. For length, simply measure length of book and add 2". Cut fabric and interfacing to measurement. Press

interfacing onto fabric. Press ½" over on each end of your width. Stitch.

Fold piece in half and press lightly to get sense of center.

Use book again to fold edges over book edges and close book completely. Make sure insides are same measurement. Mark that measurement; fold and press. Flip cover over and fold insides back, matching right sides together (A). Mark and pin length of book on both sides, adding extra ⅜". Be sure both sides are evenly matched with each other. Fold top and bottom part of middle and press (B). Sew along edges. Trim any excess fabric and turn jacket inside out (C). Press again with a

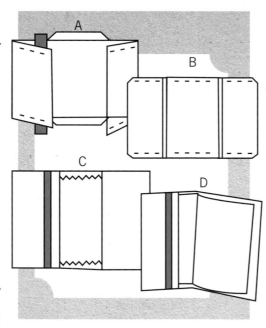

steam iron. If buckling appears with the interfacing, press firmly with iron for several minutes. Insert journal covers into the pockets (D).

JEWELRY BOX

(Page 70-71)

Materials

- ⅛" book board
- Craft glue
- Decorative paper
- Foam brush
- Kraft brown paper
- Newspaper print 19" x 27": 1 sheet
- Ruler
- Scissors
- Triangle
- X-acto knife

Instructions

Cut eight pieces of book board (E):

—2 long strips: 1½" x 9⅞"
—2 long strips: 1½" x 9⅞"
—1 box tray base: 4½" x 10½"
—2 cover pieces: 4¾" x 10½"
—1 spine piece: 1 9⁄16" x 10½"

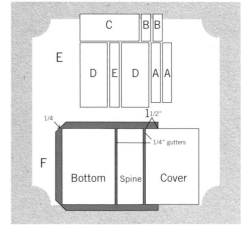

Assemble box using pieces A, B, and C by gluing edges (E). Make sure walls are straight.

Assemble base, spine, and cover with D and E. Lay down cut kraft brown paper enough to cover all base and spine and 1¼" of cover. Give 1" extra on top, side, and bottom for folding (F). Vertical cuts in corners will

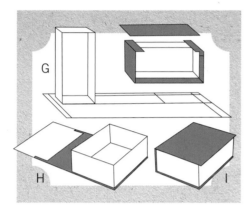

allow paper to be folded in. Trim any excess paper on corners before folding for a cleaner look. If some areas dry before folding, apply a bit of glue to keep paper wet.

Cut base corners for easy folding. Apply glue across brown kraft paper with foam brush and place pieces, allowing ¼" gutter in between. Fold edges in, around three sides.

Glue decorative paper to cover using same technique; fold edges in and cut another piece for inside cover.

Cut two 4" x 11" strips of decorative paper and glue to cover sides of base. Fold in edges and inside. Cut to size another piece to fit inside base (G).

Glue one side and base of box and attach to outside cover (H).

Press firmly and place books on top while drying process is complete (I).

LAUNDRY BAG

(Pages 76-77)

Materials
• Buttons or sequins
• Fabric
• Iron and ironing board
• Iron-on transfer
• Sewing scissors
• Straight pins
• Twisted cording

Instructions
Cut one piece of fabric 13" x 35". Fold ½" to wrong side along each long edge and press. Sew along folded edge, 2½" down from each short end.

Fold each short end ½" to wrong side and press. Fold same edge, down 2" to wrong side again, and pin. Sew across each end 1" down from folded edge.

Sew across 2" from edge to make a casing for cording.

With right sides facing, fold, piece in half crosswise. Sew side edges together, leaving casing edges unsewn.

Cut two pieces of twisted cording, each 36" long. Thread cording pieces through casings on front and back pieces and knot ends together to secure.

Iron on transfer image of choice. Image on transfer should be reversed and apply firm pressure when ironing. Follow manufacturer recommendations. Embellish with buttons or sequins and hand sew a large stitch along edges of image.

HANGER COVERS

(Page 78)

Materials
• 1" buttons
• Fabric
• Hangers
• Iron and ironing board
• Fabric marker
• Scissors
• Sewing machine
• Sewing scissors
• Straight pins

Instructions
Cut rectangle of fabric to 16½" x 15½". Make buttonhole 1" wide at center. Fold rectangle in half, right side together, so that buttonhole is at top. Place hanger on top for guide and trace outer edge on fabric with fabric marker. Sew both sides, trim to ½". Turn right side out and press. Hem on bottom and slip cover over hanger.

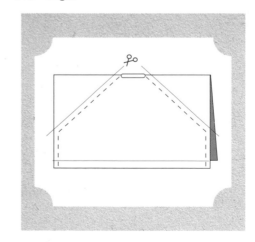

CLOTHESPIN BAGS

(Page 79)

Materials
- Fabric
- Iron and ironing board
- Sewing machine
- Sewing scissors
- Small wooden hanger

Instructions

Cut fabric to width of hanger an add 1". Stitch down contrasting fabric on right side of bag fabric. Cut pocket open and clip into corners. Turn excess contrast fabric in and stitch down along edge. Fold very top edges of bag piece over ½", press and stitch down. Fold bag piece, matching right sides together, and stitch down along edges at ½". Leave top 1" open for hanger. Turn and press. Insert hanger through pocket.

SINK SKIRT

(Pages 80-81)

Materials
- Fabric
- Hook-and-loop tape (optional)
- Iron and ironing board
- Pushpins (optional)
- Sewing machine
- Sewing marker

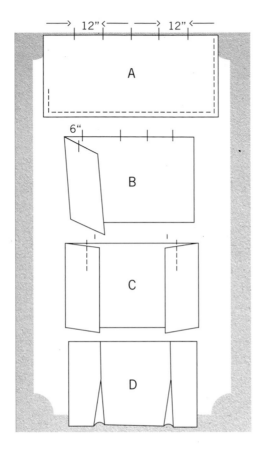

Instructions

Measure under sink space to determine length and width needed. For each pleat desired, include extra 12" of fabric (A). Cut fabric 2" wider and 4" longer than finished measurements. Hem sides and bottom of fabric. Mark center at top of fabric. Measure out from center to placement of desired pleat. Allow 12" in between each pleat. Match these placements by folding fabric over—you should have 6" between fold and markings (B). Pin along 6" in from edge for pleat, until about ⅓ way down (C). Press edge down length of fabric.

Stitch down pleat along pinned line (D). Repeat for any other pleats. Flatten pleat by opening it up and matching pressed edge to your seam. Press open and baste. Measure from edge in for an even pleat line along length of fabric. Use pressed line in recessed pleat as centering line. Hem top. You should have 2" to attach under or over sink space. Either tack it underneath sink with pushpins (if there is a wood frame) or attach skirt to outside of porcelain with heavy-duty hook-and-loop tape.

ÉTAGÈRE

(Pages 94-95)

Materials
- Cardstock: natural (2 per crate)
- Craft glue or spray adhesive
- Old seed packets or vintage labels
- Outdoor paint: color of choice
- Paintbrush: large
- Sandpaper
- Wooden pine crates: 12" x 10" x 20"

Instructions

Note: Boxes made out of ¼"-thick pine can be purchased at crafts store.

To make your étagère, paint it with your choice of color (nettle or thistle hues are garden favorites). Let paint dry at least 30 minutes. Sand edges lightly for a worn effect. Color copy old seed packets or vintage labels onto 8" x 10" natural cardstock. Using craft glue or spray adhesive, mount cardstock to sides of crate; let dry completely.

FLOWER PRESS

(Pages 96-97)

Materials
- ⅛"-thick chipboard
- ⅝" buckles: 4
- ⅝" ribbon
- Blotting paper
- Cardboard
- Craft glue
- Cutting knife
- Fabric
- Scissors
- Sewing machine

Instructions

Cut two pieces of chipboard to 8" x 6¾". Apply craft glue to wrong side of 9" x 7" fabric piece and place one of chipboard pieces on top. Cut corners diagonally and fold each side over; cut excess fabric at corners; let dry 3-4 hours.

Cut nine pieces of cardboard and 16 pieces of blotting paper to 8" x 6¼". Layer two blotting papers between each cardboard.

Once fabric is dry, place two strips of ribbon 22" long about 5" apart, centered on one chipboard; adhere with glue. Put flowers between sheets of blotting paper. (Place cardboards and blotting paper and chipboard with the fabric on top). Fold ribbon over and either tie each one or use ⅝" buckles. Pull ribbon taut to ensure firm pressing.

Note: If attaching buckles, feed each ribbon through two buckles and sew end onto the ribbon itself. The other end of the ribbon will be used to secure the flower press.

HERB CARDS & BOX

(Page 98)

Materials
- Acrylic paint
- Cardstock or cardboard
- Craft glue
- Fine-point pen: black
- Garden snips
- Paper tape
- Scissors
- Small box: cardboard or wooden
- Spray adhesive
- Fresh herbs: sage, rosemary, lavender

Instructions

To make box: Paint inside and outside of wooden box with acrylic paint; let dry. Photocopy templates of small herbal frames onto cardstock (see Archives, pages 102-113). Cover back side of image with spray adhesive; attach to top of box. **Note:** You can enlarge or shrink these to fit your box.

To make herb cards: Cut desired number of cards same dimension of inside of box. Snip short cuttings of herbs or small flowers and tape onto cards on top and bottom of specimen. Label each card with herb's name.

GARDEN APRON

(Page 100)

Materials
- Fabric 27½" x 9" (for pocket)
- Fabric: 27½" x 15" (for base)
- Floral fabric 8" x 9" (for pocket)
- Iron and ironing board
- Measuring tape
- Ribbon: 18"
- Sewing maching
- Sewing scissors

Instructions

To make pockets: Measure pocket fabric into thirds, leaving extra inch on either side for hemming.

Sew floral fabric onto middle section with basting stitch, by machine or hand, as close to edge as possible.

Cover sides of floral fabric with ribbon, covering basting stitch. Sew down inner edge of ribbon on either side of floral only. Hem top edge of pockets.

To make base: Line up bottom of pocket fabric with base fabric. Baste two pieces together along outer edges.

Stitch along outer edges of accent ribbon to form three pockets. Hem outer edges. Fold over top ½" then stitch down ties. Fold over width of ties then hem.

To make ties: Cut two pieces of fabric 5" x desired length. Fold each edge over ½"; press. Fold in half, press, and then stitch ties to apron.

Kaari Meng grew up in Southern California in a close-knit family that encouraged creative spirits. Collecting, cake decorating, pottery, and jewelry making filled her early days.

In college she studied government, graduating with a Bachelor of Arts degree from the University of San Francisco in 1988. During her college years, Kaari traveled around Europe, living in London for a semester to work in the House of Commons.

In her early 20s, fresh out of college, Kaari moved to New York City and worked at the Metropolitan Museum of Art, where she met her husband, Jon.

In 1990, Kaari went back to school at the Fashion Institute of Technology in New York City and studied jewelry-making techniques. Her first company, Kaari Meng Designs, specialized in designing and making vintage glass jewelry, which she sold to specialty shops including Anthropologie, Sundance Catalog, and Peruvian Connection.

Sofia Zabala was born in 1997, which allowed Kaari to work from home and pursue another creative outlet that had been brewing— French General.

In 1999, with a barn full of French flea market finds, Kaari and her sister, Molly, opened French General on Crosby Street in New York City. In 2003, French General moved to Hollywood, California, where Kaari and her husband Jon, purveyors of French living, run a small business creating interesting items such as laundry products, home décor accessories, and vintage beading kits sold online at **www.frenchgeneral.com** and in stores throughout the United States, Japan, Singapore, and Europe. French General also offers services including custom home textiles, interior consulting, and period decorating.

Jon, Kaari, and their daughter, Sofia, reside in Los Feliz, California.

ACKNOWLEDGMENTS

Writing this book has been a group effort. It has also allowed me to work with all sorts of wonderful artists, whom I would like to thank.

First and foremost, the person who taught me to collect and craft, my mom—Kick Meng—who pulled out her craft books as soon as she heard about a French General book project and gave us countless ideas and projects for embellishing the home. To my two sisters, Lisa and Molly, who along with my mom, spent many a day at the shop brainstorming and developing ideas. What a great session—thanks sisters! All created and contributed beautiful work to our book.

To Melissa Easton, an amazing artist who walked into our lives when French General was in New York and whose talent we've been unable to get out of our head. Thank you for the beautiful artwork—it has added a true element of the curious to our book.

To the girls at Paper Source in Pasadena, California—Joby Weber, Dariana Cruz, Sarah Corley, and Adelle Atkinson. Thank you for taking on the paper projects and bringing your unique sense of style to the pages of this book—and in record time.

To Jody Rice and Rebecca Shiraev, two of our talented sewers at French General. Thank you for your willingness to jump in and sew when there were 100 other sewing jobs to finish. Your work is much appreciated.

To my good friend, Sue Etkin, whose glass blowing and beaded glasswork has lit up my life as well as many beautiful homes and hotels throughout the world.

To Elizabeth Baer, my textile mentor, who has inspired me and filled my mind with more information and history than I could have ever imagined. Thank you for your words and your projects.

To all of the girls at French General who work on a daily basis to build this company and the concept of living with decorative crafts and textiles. Thank you Alexis Lantz, Tara Green, and Christine Shelly.

To Eileen Paulin, Cathy Risling, and Rebecca Ittner. Thanks for believing I could do this, and seeing me through 'til the bitter end. And to Zac Williams, the calm, cool photographer who captured the essence of French General.

Finally to all of my family—Dad, Mom, Lisa, David, Syra, Michael, Christy, Makayla, Logan, John, Molly, and Ryan…and mostly to Juan Carlos and our baby gal, the one who knows it all, Sofia. Thank you for giving me the benefit of the doubt and offering helping hands every step of the way while building this project known as French General. Merci!

Kaari Meng

SUPPLIERS

ADELLE ATKINSON

www.adellelouise.com
Paper crafts

THE CANDLEMAKER

www.thecandlemaker.com
Beeswax sheets

CATALINA PAINTS

www.catalinapaints.com
Paints and supplies

DARIANA CRUZ

www.folkloreye.com
Paper crafts

DULKEN & DERRICK

www.dulkenandderrick.com
Millinery flowers

ELIZABETH BAER

29 Church St., Bradford on Avon,
Wilts, BA15 1LN, U.K.
Textiles

FRENCH GENERAL

www.frenchgeneral.com
Beads, textiles, notions, laundry products

JAMES COUNTRY MERCANTILE

www.jamescountry.com
Camp stools

JOBY WEBER

E-mail: jbwhandmadebooks@gmail.com
Paper & book crafts

LE MELANGE

www.lemelange.com
Bath salts, essential oils, cotton muslin bags

MELISSA EASTON

www.melissaeastondesigns.com
Illustrations

MICHAEL'S

www.michaels.com
Magnets, milk crates, craft supplies

MOLLY MENG (8MM)

www.thatsprettyexciting.com
Collage art

PAPER SOURCE

www.paper-source.com
Gift wrap, stationery and crafts

PHOTO WEIGHTS

www.photoweights.com
Paperweights

SARA CORLEY

E-mail: saracorley@mac.com
Paper crafts

SUZAN ETKIN ART PRODUCTIONS

www.suzanetkinenterprises.com
Beaded light covers, hand blown chandeliers

TINSEL TRADING CO.

www.tinseltrading.com
Ribbon, trim, and vintage millinery

ZABALA DESIGN

www.zabaladesign.com
Print and web design

METRIC EQUIVALENCY CHARTS

INCHES TO MILLIMETERS (MM) AND CENTIMETERS (CM)

Inches	mm	cm	Inches	cm	Inches	cm
⅛	3	0.3	9	22.9	30	76.2
¼	6	0.6	10	25.4	31	78.7
½	13	1.3	12	30.5	33	83.8
⅝	16	1.6	13	33.0	34	86.4
¾	19	1.9	14	35.6	35	88.9
⅞	22	2.2	15	38.1	36	91.4
1	25	2.5	16	40.6	37	94.0
1¼	32	3.2	17	43.2	38	96.5
1½	38	3.8	18	45.7	39	99.1
1¾	44	4.4	19	48.3	40	101.6
2	51	5.1	20	50.8	41	104.1
2½	64	6.4	21	53.3	42	106.7
3	76	7.6	22	55.9	43	109.2
3½	89	8.9	23	58.4	44	111.8
4	102	10.2	24	61.0	45	114.3
4½	114	11.4	25	63.5	46	116.8
5	127	12.7	26	66.0	47	119.4
6	152	15.2	27	68.6	48	121.9
7	178	17.8	28	71.1	49	124.5
8	203	20.3	29	73.7	50	127.0

YARDS TO METERS

yards	meters	yards	meters	yards	meters	yards	meters	yards	meters
⅛	0.11	2⅛	1.94	4⅛	3.77	6⅛	5.60	8⅛	7.43
¼	0.23	2¼	2.06	4¼	3.89	6¼	5.72	8¼	7.54
⅜	0.34	2⅜	2.17	4⅜	4.00	6⅜	5.83	8⅜	7.66
½	0.46	2½	2.29	4½	4.11	6½	5.94	8½	7.77
⅝	0.57	2⅝	2.40	4⅝	4.23	6⅝	6.06	8⅝	7.89
¾	0.69	2¾	2.51	4¾	4.34	6¾	6.17	8¾	8.00
⅞	0.80	2⅞	2.63	4⅞	4.46	6⅞	6.29	8⅞	8.12
1	0.91	3	2.74	5	4.57	7	6.40	9	8.23
1⅛	1.03	3⅛	2.86	5⅛	4.69	7⅛	6.52	9⅛	8.34
1¼	1.14	3¼	2.97	5¼	4.80	7¼	6.63	9¼	8.46
1⅜	1.26	3⅜	3.09	5⅜	4.91	7⅜	6.74	9⅜	8.57
1½	1.37	3½	3.20	5½	5.03	7½	6.86	9½	8.69
1⅝	1.49	3⅝	3.31	5⅝	5.14	7⅝	6.97	9⅝	8.80
1¾	1.60	3¾	3.43	5¾	5.26	7¾	7.09	9¾	8.92
1⅞	1.71	3⅞	3.54	5⅞	5.37	7⅞	7.20	9⅞	9.03
2	1.83	4	3.66	6	5.49	8	7.32	10	9.14

INDEX

French General